Life or Death
in Satan's Swamp

The Final Installment of the Trump Card Series

--

Imagine, if you can, that time travel was possible and that all ancient prophecy is not prediction, but merely a recounting of events that have already happened.

Imagine, if you can, the need to confirm that the travel experiment was a success. If you change history, those who exist where you began would not know it – they might not even exist in the time which emerged after the changes that you made.

More important, in the newly created timeline, you might not exist – for theorists, it's a *"temporal paradox."*

But what if you created a vaguely worded prophecy?

Then, possibly, tied it to the mathematics of a calendar system. If you emerged too close to the event, might you *"Bury the Lede"* and scramble the thoughts in books that are related to those where you exposed the *"prophetic"* method you used?

Fact becomes fiction, fiction yields to fact, mythology is revealed to be archaeological history in story form. And, the beauty of it is, while you have made yourself known, you have not altered that which gave rise to your existence.

Set right premise and you can turn history into a novel that is written before the history occurs.

This is the final book in the Trump Card series – But, we could postulate that the adventure is only about to begin.

Be vary careful. If you understand what is being said, you could change history – if you did, is it possible that you would also push some travelers into a *"Temporal Paradox?"*

Did I just present an *"elevator pitch"* for a sci-fi novel, or did I reveal what was actually happening in 2021?

CHAPTERS

CHAPTER ONE –Start a New Era

2020/21, became the years in which entering a bank wearing a mask, walking up to a telling and requesting or demanding money, was both legal and proper.

The year 2021 began with Donald John Trump challenging the validity of the election results. As could be expected, those who welcomed the 2016 results with calls to impeach the winner are now calling for a criminal investigation of Trump because he showed the audacity to challenge the fact their candidate appears to have won.

As mentioned in Book 11 of this series, Joe Biden won for the same reason Trump defeated Clinton in 2016 – a kinship connection to the 4-Sisters, which every POTUS has had, and a POTUS Cousin connection to the other seated Presidents.

Hillary's only link to the family bloodline dynasty was as First Lady and mother of a POTUS Cousin; Trump's connection is that of a POTUS Cousin father and a descendant of two of the 4-Sisters; Biden is a POTUS Cousin, descended from three of the 4-Sisters.

In the chain of preference, Trump trumped Clinton, and then Biden trumped Trump. The next issue of national significance shall be Biden's replacement – neither Kamala Harris, Ted Cruz, or Mike Pence are members of the historic bloodline.

Look to Spain in 1492, France in 1789, or Germany in 1931. We can ignore Russia – it has always held a place on the edge of the dynastic line and in that role served as an eastern border controlling Eastern territories of possible future value.

Of the three primary nations, each held a position of power or leadership until it decided to compete with a nation of greater ancestral connection. At that point, there was a revolution. And after the Revolution, the mobs severed the connection between the blood and state, and the nation never really recovered.

Only Britain managed to escape the dynastic fate. And then, it did so by creating a constitutional monarchy of descendants of the 4-Sisters – which included having descendants serve as a House of Lords. Those who were not in line for a Title found other means of showing their importance or relevance – some lead settlers to the New World and set the seeds for the POTUS Cousins. Once here, members of the line went into many areas. Some became political or educational leaders, others went into the Theater and you'd be surprised at how many of the best know stars of the Silver Screen are also POTUS Cousins.

Apart from the genealogy that was first revealed by the 1981 publication of *"Burke's Presidential Families of the United States of America,"* only my books have gone a step further and pointed out a common ancestry that goes beyond the Presidents having noble ancestors.

More significantly, it was only through *"Jonathon's POTUS COUSINS"* that you learned of a shared common or interconnected kinships; only via this series did we all discover that every President has been a direct descendant of Charlemagne the Great via 4-Sisters born in the 1170s. Throughout European history, whenever there is a conflict, a nation lead by descendants of Charlemagne has defeated the nation lead by a usurper.

Talking about "Democracy" is much like discussing a Biblical tribal system of the type attributed to Moses. The Tribes ruled their own territory, but under to control of the Levites and Kohanim who had "no inheritance" in the land – but ruled over all the tribes.

When Greece conquered Israel, Alexander the Great showed great respect for the Hebrew culture and traditions – so much so that the name "Alexander" became Jewish. Then, Rome replaced Greece and introduced a disrespect for the Levites, Israel vanished – Palestine was created in its place.

As we know, a Jewish man, a relative of the High Priests who, even as a child, could walk freely through the inner chambers of the Temple, emerged and gained a following that was a threat to Rome – so Rome had him crucified and placed the blame on unidentified members of a mob who were designated Jewish but, in reality, were simply supplicants of the Roman leadership.

In Europe, whenever descendants of Charlemagne ceased to hold or were violently removed from, power, the significance of the nation appears to have declined – unless bolstered by a nation ruled by the descendants.

It seems silly. And those who would rather live in denial of history and documented ancestry would reject the factual pattern.

America is now in the process of testing the hypothesis whose evidence is found in the genealogy and related election results over the past 230 years. But then, they make it a point to avoid reading *"Jonathon's POTUS COUSINS."*

Possibly the greatest threat to modern democratic culture is the impact of systemic disinformation propagated by Main Stream Media {MSM} and those who abuse Social Media – either as corrupt actors, or the censors who create the *"communication guidelines."*

Disinformation has been with us for as long as humans have relied on *"myth, rumor, or gossip."* The disinformation foundation preceded the story of "The Emperor's New Clothes" which only the "wise" could see, and relies on the herd instinct or need to conform to the common belief. It is a hostile virus that dominates certain environments and thrives by corrupting the human mind.

As predicted in the title of my March 2014 book *"Death Over Life: Secret of Revelation: A Prophecy of America's Destruction"*, in 2016 the nation entered a phase where the citizens would decide if they want the *"Great American Experiment"* to continue or self-destruct.

Information and belief systems define the nature of societies and cultures. We stereotype those who are different or are deemed to be the "other," the "outsider" and in doing so, we effectively create the stereotype by which we are to be known.

Those who control the flow of information and its character represent the power that shapes domestic and foreign relationships through the shaping of attitudes which can then be weaponized to the point of irrationality.

Early in his campaign, Donald Trump voiced the idea that he could shoot someone on Fifth Avenue and it would have no effect on his base. In 2018, Joseph Biden bragged about his spearheading an Obama approved *quid pro quo* blackmailing of Ukraine's President to have their Prosecutor General fired – and, even while the House Democrats were yelling Trump should be impeached for an alleged *quid pro quo* request for information – as authorized by the 1998 Clinton Treaty with Ukraine – those same House Democrats were saying Biden would be the 2020 Democratic nominee. And they were saying it even before the candidates were announced.

Just three weeks before the November 3rd election, with the early voting already registering nearly 20 million ballots filed, there was an email revelation that explicitly affirmed that Hunter Biden had been engaged to arrange for an end to the Burisma investigation being conducted by the Prosecutor General that Joe Biden – with the stated authorization of President Barack Obama – would force to be fired.

The disinformation policy invoked was based on attacking the character insulting the Prosecutor General – yet, when has America ever fired a secondary foreign official? We know that the American government has engaged in "regime change" and the Vietnam War serves as a model for attempts to deny foreign citizens the right to the government of their choosing.

But, to fire an Attorney General? Especially one engaged in fighting corruption within their nation? When have we ever done that? It seems only when the Vice President's son is receiving a million dollars a year and – as his email to his daughter revealed – splitting the proceeds with his father.

But those seem to be "Facts" and as Biden has declared – he prefers "Truth over Fact" and his "Truth" is based on disinformation or obfuscation of facts. And leading up to the election, 57-percent of voters polled indicated they prefer the disinformation to the facts – even when it is the candidate who brags about the facts.

Alexis de Tocqueville visited America in 1831 and then wrote of what he observed about the American Election system; 190 years later and nothing has changed – though, much to the chagrin of traditional politicians, Donald John Trump has been reshaping or upsetting the ancient pattern described here:

"Long before the appointed day arrives, the election becomes the greatest, and one might say the only, affair occupying men's minds... The President, for his part, is absorbed in the task of defending himself before the majority... As the election draws near, intrigues grow more active and agitation is more lively and widespread. The citizens divide up into several camps... The whole nation gets into a feverish state. ..."

Was Trump become absorbed in his own defense?

Or, is it that he kept redrawing the lines in such a way as to render it imperative that he be attacked – even before he was sworn in?

There is a rule I believe I invented and have lived by since I was a child: *"Always play by the other guy's rules; that way, when you win, he has no right to bitch."* Though, experience shows those defeated by their own rules are always seem to be the ones who bitch and scream the loudest.

Well. OK. I might not have invented it, but I do believe I was the first to codify it as an expression. If we look at Congress, we see that they tend to live by the rule without any idea of what they are doing.

Think about the "Birther movement" – the idea that Barack Obama was born in Kenya and not in the United States; inherent in the idea is that his pregnant mother left his father in Hawaii and flew to Kenya to give birth, did not seek to record the birth with the embassy there, but, instead smuggled baby Barack onto some mode of international transportation, and then circumvented customs at her port-of-entry.

Meanwhile, back in Hawaii, his Kenyan father was apparently arranging with Records Officials to falsely record the birth in their local records and then include it in the media report they regularly issued.

Gee! How many people believed that was done – rather than just giving birth at the local hospital or wherever?

That Republican fantasy was invented so that there would be a basis to remove Obama from office. But the Republicans didn't have anyone stupid enough to place their name on a legislation that would place the fantasy in the Congressional record for legislative action.

Enter Donald Trump, who defies the polls and defeats Hillary via the Electoral College. Immediately, Democrats begin to scream that the election was stolen and the Russia was to blame. So they yell election fraud and the first move to impeach is submitted before the 2017 Inauguration. As a result, we have four years of President Trump trying to do his job and the House of Representatives trying to impeach him for things like obeying a treaty with Ukraine.

If the Republicans can attempt to remove Obama, why is it not right for the Democrats to remove Trump? And since there was a call to *"Lock Her Up"* leveled against Hillary Clinton, why not have the continual calls to toss "private citizen" Trump in jail?

Wouldn't be a historic landmark to have the first-ever 2nd impeachment of a President capped off with his being convicted as a private citizen and then also convicted of imaginary civil crimes?

What better way to ensure Trump's eternal place in history? Even failure achieves that end.

Trump brought the first Orthodox Jewish family members (daughter Ivanka Trump and son-in-law Jared Kushner) into the White House, and now Kamala Harris brings with her the first second gentleman – who happens to be Jewish, so another first. If Trump escapes crimes farce – we can describe the outcome in terms of an old Jewish joke: *"They tried to kill us, we survived, let's eat."*

As with all Catholic attacks on Jews, Pelosi decided that the last days of the Trump Administration should be a second attempt to impeach. Which Trump might eventually come to describe with *"They tried to destroy me, they failed, let's play golf."*

Of course, the cycle must be full, so the 2020 election saw the fraud charge revolve around behavior caused by the Coronavirus – mail-in ballots, no proper identification of voters, indications of the ballots being used to vote multiple times or on behalf of the dead.

There was a record turnout – people did not need to find time to stand in line at a polling place, they could vote early by mail. But, we know there are always irregularities; there is a history of voter suppression, vote manipulation, or flat out cheating, that is easily as old as the nation. If the Democrats could yell Russia when Trump won, it seems proper that Trump should yell about well-known sets of irregularities that accompany every election.

There is always truth in routine traditional "fraud," the real issue is the pandemic and the lack of verifiable in-person voting. It is not something we should want to risk in future elections.

But, if Congress doesn't care to ensure Ballot Box security, is it something we should care about? Impeaching Trump twice is far more fun, and easier to do. But then, Biden bragged of the doing the *Quid Pro Quo* the Democrats claimed was an impeachable offense, so it follows that the circle should be completed and Biden should now be impeached – using Democratic standards opposed to *Quid Pro Quo* pressure of a foreign government.

But what of the pandemic?

By October 2020, the nation had seen an imaginary pandemic – what Trump had defined as a "Hoax" – *a humorous or malicious deception* – whose deceptive nature came in the defining of a culling virus as some deadly thing to be feared when, in fact, it was just a disruptive passenger inciting the true killer to act faster.

One of the issues with Covid-19 is the emerging evidence that many severe and long-lasting symptoms of COVID-19 are driven by autoimmunity, a condition where the immune system turns against the body. And this makes Covid-19 the ideal virus for a nation that is turning against itself – turning its use of legal codes against the very nature and purpose of its laws or Constitution.

In a way, even that reality fits a de Tocqueville observation of a nation where "...*everyone thinks he has an interest in furnishing proof of an offense and in arresting the guilty man.*"

Granted, we can more easily observe it in the "Lock Her Up" cries that were dogging Hillary Clinton in 2016 and as the election approached were resurrected with the revelation that she planned and paid for the Russian Hoax – in a context where both President Barack Obama and Vice President Joseph Biden enjoyed what the documentary evidence reveals was full knowledge of the events and presumptively gave their full consent.

As we know, Biden bragged of his felony violation of multiple articles of 18USC – again, asserting the full knowledge and consent of Obama. In an honest world, a world outside of politics, a confession like that would earn Biden anywhere from 6 to 20 years in prison. But in modern America, Donald Trump was attacked for invoking the Clinton-era United States and Ukraine treaty providing for an exchange of investigative findings. Specifically, a request for any Burisma investigation findings that mention either Joseph or Hunter Biden.

It would seem de Tocqueville was correct about those who believe they have "*an interest in furnishing proof of an offense and in arresting the guilty man*" – many have investigated and sought proof. But for President Trump, it is a constitutional responsibility to follow-up on a public confession to a Federal felony. And it seems it is now the obligation of The House of Representatives to negate that responsibility by making it a crime to investigate a crime.

Of course, they could not come out and charge Trump with the crime of investigating a confession of criminal activity; this meant we were given the entertaining spectacle of impeachment without a stated statutory crime or misdemeanor. One in which the witnesses claimed the criminal was the Ukraine Prosecutor General who was leading the Burisma investigation.

We can set aside the fact Biden's blackmailing of the Ukraine

President also violated Ukrainian law – that's their problem.

Thanks to court documents related to felony charges against Hunter's partner, we now have hard evidence that Hunter received from Burisma over $83 thousand a month for seventeen months – and we know the purpose was to lobby to keep the Americans from joining the corruption investigation into Burisma. Something Joe Biden assisted with.

But, as far as *"arresting the guilty man"*? Americans have a better idea – make him the 46th President and enjoy whatever new and improved corruption can emerge from the political swamp.

But what of the 'Hoax" that defines the American aspect of the Covid-19 pandemic?

As the first germs reached American shores, Biden declared Trump was displaying *"xenophobic racism"* because he was shutting down the borders to all but citizens returning home.

Faced with a virus that had Chinese connections as its roots and origin, House Speaker Nancy Pelosi made a point to encourage superspreader gatherings in San Francisco's Chinatown.

At the same time, as the virus was raging through Europe, in New York City, Mayor Bill De Blasio was encouraging people to act normal and he would wait seven months before he would require those arriving from Europe to self-quarantine. Of course, by then New York had passed its virus epicenter phase, and those passing through the eats coast travel hub had infected most of the nation.

This impacted the poor or minority neighborhoods to a great extent. We can therefore assume these people will be the ones to back Biden for, as de Tocqueville phrased it:

"The poor man retains the prejudices of his forefathers without their faith, and their ignorance without their virtues; he has adopted the doctrine of self-interest as the rule of his actions, without understanding the science which puts it to use; and his selfishness is no less blind than was formerly his devotedness to others."

The prejudice of the poor is a hatred for the rich and all who have risen out of poverty. The millionaire politician likes to speak of their lower-class roots. The Presidents can often do that. But they all share a common ancestor in Emperor Charlemagne and in the 4-Sisters who were his descendants. Break that connection, and the nation will fall – and that fall of the nation is what profits those who back Biden, who has said that, if the Doctors say to lockdown the nation, he would.

But that's where the hoax emerges.

Are you going to lockdown the nation because people smoke?

Ok, you don't get it. But that's simply because you haven't asked about the comparative reality.

We all grew-up seeing people smoke. Most people are aware that neither Biden nor Trump are smokers. But how many know that smoking kills over 480 thousand people every year?

Where are the draconian measures, the lockdowns and masks to protect against second hand smoke and the quarantining of those who are active smokers?

As of 11 October, which was 41 weeks into the year, Covid-19 was cited in the deaths of about 219 thousand. If the average death rate remanded constant, that would be about 278 thousand deaths for the year – or about 58% of the number who die from a product available for sale to everyone over the age of 18.

People have the right to pay to create or be among the 9.2 thousand a week who die from smoking every year; as with Covid-19, smoking kills more men than women and that ensures women will outlive men.

But those are just American CDC numbers, if we look at the World Health Organization website, we discover: *"Tobacco kills more than 8 million people each year. More than 7 million of those deaths are the result of direct tobacco use while around 1.2 million are the result of non-smokers being exposed to second-hand smoke."*

The website also informs us that *"Tobacco kills up to half of its users."* And *"Over 80% of the world's 1.3 billion tobacco users live in low- and middle-income countries."*

So we are in a panic over a culling virus that has killed just over 1 million people in 41 weeks, and don't care about having killed *"8 million people each year."*

The CDC informs us that *"In 2018, tobacco companies spent $9.06 billion marketing cigarettes and smokeless tobacco in the United States. This amount translates to about $25 million each day, or more than $1 million every hour. Cigarette advertising and* *promotional expenses totaled approximately $8.4 billion in 2018—a decrease from 2017.*"

In exchange for all that advertising, "*A $5 pack-a-day habit costs a smoker nearly $2,000 a year.*" So people pay $2,000 every year for a chance to be among the 9.2 thousand a week who will die – whatever the odds, wouldn't it be far more intelligent to use that money to buy a weekly lottery ticket?

For those concerned with Climate Change, elimination of the Tobacco farming and CO_2 or other poisonous gases related to that industry would do wonders.

Granted, we hear the media promoting larger death numbers in the USA over the next two largest – India and Brazil – but the 2020 life expectancy for India was 69.73 years, a 0.33% increase from 2019; for Brazil, 75.96 years, a 0.27% increase from 2019; for the USA it was 78.93 years, a 0.08% increase from 2019. As we know, the older the population the more deaths. That means that the American life expectancy is working to enhance the numbers – a fact that carries into the deaths in European nations whose life expectancy exceeds that of the USA.

The weirdness in the WHO data indicates newborns in China can expect 68.7 years of healthy life, while in America they can look forward to 68.5 years. This equates to a Life expectancy of 76.96 for those Chinese who exceed expectations – thus an average Chinese baby lives a few months longer than their American counterpart but having done so, will die about 2.4 years before an American.

Those nations with shorter life expectancies will have fewer Covid-19 deaths.

Remember, Covid-19 is a culling virus that affects those over 75, and if you do not live that long, it isn't going to kill you – because you are already dead.

Another fun metric – if the average age of the population is low, the percentage of the population that dies from Covid-19 will be lower. But then we have the issue of suicide.

The National Institute of Mental Health reported a steady rise in suicide among the young through the last two years of Obama into the first two trump years – suicide is the second-highest cause of death among the young. Will Biden's health care choices see fit to address this problem? Or will Biden repeat the Obama era choices that brought it on?

One of the ongoing realities that MSM will need to deal with is the persistence of Donald Trump.

Professional Politicians deem him a problem – he does not bow to their criminal conduct. The Democrats have shown just how scared they are of him, he's a person capable of repeating the double election of Grover Cleveland and he has made it know that he might for a third-party, a Patriot's Party, that would place him on an equal par with a 11912 Theodore Roosevelt.

In 1912, the third-party was the "*Progressive Party*" founded on what Roosevelt would call the "*Square Deal*" and the Roosevelt wing was colloquially known as the "*Bull Moose Party*."

We tend to forget that the programs we now associate with Democrats came into being through a combination of the Great Depression and the election of Franklin Delano Roosevelt – FDR being Teddy's cousin who was married to yet another cousin.

If we set aside the problem of age, the Swamp Denizens are aware that Donald could succeed where Teddy failed. And Donald most certainly could echo Cleveland's success.

Donald is, in terms of the GOP Swamp, pure poison. But for the GOP base, he's the Messiah, and those politicians who would like to continue working in Washington know they need Donald's full support – even if he does not run again.

There are only so many lies Pelosi's Swamp critters can tell about Donald. True, it's a Kafkaesque variation on *The Emperor's New Clothes*, the fools will accept the lies and distortions – they will see what is not there and showed that when they were told in the first Impeachment that the evidence was "*overwhelming*" and yet there was no evidence to be presented before the senate.

With the historic second impeachment, the House didn't even bother with the charade – there was no evidence and no witnesses and, as we will see, the whole process was unconstitutional. But that shows just how sacred of Donald John Trump the Swamp really is.

The comical part, as you were told in the first two books in this series, was that the Progressives were conned into siding with the Swamp. Had they played the karate master, had they not fought against Trump but used his visions to transform government into an economically sound Progressive regime, they could easily have had everything they desired and received a bit more.

CHAPTER TWO – Climate

"I've come to the conclusion that historians and cardiologists are in the same boat, both trying to warn people about ingrained, destructive habits, both frequently ignored and likely with the same outcomes."
~ 11 January Tweet by Jelani Cobb

Global Warming and related Climate Change are issues that are both recognized and ignored by society. They can be seen as constituting the Hippopotamus standing next to the *Elephant in the Room* that relates to both human migration patterns and the related conflicts. The relationship is rather interesting, and it was only on 6 January that I saw it interns of the books I've written over the past two decades.

The trigger event was reading an article that mentioned the Medieval Warming Period and cited an era of about 150-years which matched the period I have calculated – in my 2014 book, *"thinking about Biblical Prophecy: Are we in the Revelation Era"* – as the end of the first thousand year era cited in *Revelation* 20:7-8. This is the point in history where Satan is unbound to create a militaristic era that conforms to the rise of the Vikings.

The progenitor of all our Presidents, Charlemagne the Great, was born around 742, became King of the Franks, and created all the major European nations. The Vikings arose in the same period, and their raids are dated to 795. Which creates a pattern of two forces carving out territory during the same era. As the climate warmed, the Vikings headed west and, around 980, settled Greenland and quite likely reached the Americas.

The Medieval Warm Period (MWP) is believed to have begun about 114 years after his death – or about two 57-year cycles after his death. He died in 814, and the MWP is said to have begun between 900 and 950. This places the MWP about seventeen 56-year periods (952 years) from the beginning of our calendar. Double that cycle, and we have the year 1904 – roughly the start of the current phase of Global warming. The prophecy fails to provide a starting date – our calendar wasn't created from the Hebrew one until our year 525 – rounding to one thousand allows the starting date to be the beginning of our calendar, the year of the crucifixion, or when the *Book of Revelation* is said to have been written.

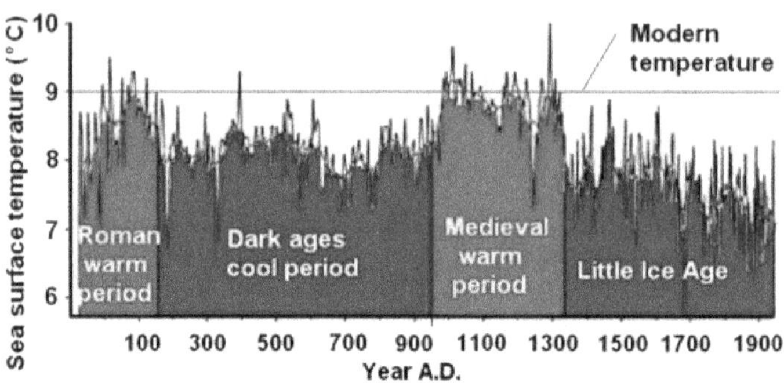

If we follow the science, MWP becomes one in a long series of warming periods corresponding to various major turning points in history. As we see on the chart, the period when Revelation was written was a period of warm and therefore military expansionism. Not shown is the fact that construction of Stonehenge and then the Pyramids was also conducted in a warming period. Later, the era associated with the Exodus also fell in a militaristic warming period.

As the chart reveals, the current warming exceeds the historic levels and foretells an era of far greater cultural change than every before.

The period of Global warming we are now experiencing can be seen as cyclically appropriate for a natural warming cycle; it has been exacerbated by the effects of the burning of fossil fuels during the Industrial Revolution and the subsequent enhanced use of wood, coal, oil, and natural gas to heat homes and workplaces for a rapidly expanding population.

As has been pointed out many times, atmospheric heat has grown in parallel to the growth in population. And, unless people change their energy patterns – or die off – the planet will continue to become warmer. With that warmth will come human migration from regions that are overheated – the regions within 15 degrees of the equator – and this will spawn cultural and military conflicts that could trigger a World War (or Biblical Apocalypse) sometime within the next two decades. The Revelation Prophecy calculations place that war in 2033.

Growing up in the 1950s, one of the great fears was another petty conflict that became a Global Nuclear War. Apart from the "Duck and Cover" drills hiding under a desk in school, there was the reports that a nuclear conflict would create a Nuclear Winter.

People shake their heads and ignore the ramifications, while

Hollywood produces endless variations on an extinction of humanity or some variation on the 2015 post-apocalyptic comedy television series "Last Man on Earth," which shared its title with the 1964 Vincent Price disease spawned zombie film. Mel Gibson's career emerged from "The Road Warrior" (1981) and gave rise to the "Mad Max" franchise.

Global holocausts are entertaining – but, they should never be taken seriously. After all, doesn't the Book of Revelation tell us that we are now in the age (2,000-years after Christ) when a third of life will die? Now, who do you know who actually lives according to the Bible and refuses to do to their neighbor anything they would not happily accept being done to or for them?

Think of America.

The MSM is upset because foreign businessmen and officials stay at a 5-star Washington hotel – just because, when Trump was playing real estate oligarch, while preserving and enhancing all its historic features, he transformed the iconic Washington, D.C. Old Post Office Pavilion into a modern luxury hotel.

But the same MSM is silent over the laptop-email evidence, and corroborative testimony of Hunter Biden's criminally convicted former partners, that Hunter leveraged his father's position as both Senator and Vice President for family gain – including evidence that both he and his siblings shared their gains with their father, Joseph R. Biden.

And apart from making a teenage girl famous for her effort to enlighten people to the risks or ramifications of Global Warming, the media has generally ignored the reality that we are well past any point-of-no-return action.

More important, if there really is a prospect of nuclear war with an ensuing nuclear winter, the wisest thing society could do is to continue the efforts toward renewables – which are also point-of-use energy sources like solar and wind power – and encourage nature to continue its global warming.

That warming would offset any harm from a nuclear winter and effectively serve to stabilize global temperatures during and immediately after a global nuclear war. A widespread renewable energy availability would also ensure that communications and data are persevered.

This is important from both a strategic military view and to ensure the average home has enough energy to maintain a relatively normal (if locked down) lifestyle. Covid-19 has served to prepared us for surviving a year-long holocaust lockdown situation; it has also establishing the experience needed to ensure a remote or virtual implementation of education and work that would ensure a rapid recovery after the nuclear effects have dissipated.

But, even though Israel's energy minister stated it would take Iran around six months to produce enough fissile material for a single nuclear weapon, it would take more than one nuclear weapon for them to risk a nuclear war. Still, as of 2 February 2021, that six month timeframe was twice as long as was anticipated by Antony Blinken, Biden's newly confirmed U.S. Secretary of State.

As we know, Trump pulled out of the Obama era 2015 Iranian nuclear deal which had allowed Iran to experiment with fissionable material so long as they did not stockpile sufficient weapons grade material before 2025.

The fact that Iran could reasonably be expected produce a weapon within months of Trump leaving office is a clear indication that they were developing the technology the Obama era deal served no meaningful purpose.

When Biden was declare to be the next President, there was excitement among Iran's leadership, who see Biden as a weak leader who is a potential savior of the Obama-era Iranian nuclear deal – a deal that would given them more time to experiment and develop a range of efficient compact nuclear weapons that will not need missile delivery systems.

Now, by enriching uranium to 20 percent, which is about 90 percent of the level required to get to weapons grade, Iran is only one technical step away from producing weapons-grade material needed for an atomic bomb.

When the Obama-Biden administration made its deal, it also transferred $1.7 billion to Iran – in foreign currency, $400 million of which was delivered by plane, stacked on wooden pallets. The need to bribe the Iranian government showed a level of weakness, or desperation, Iran anticipates will mark the Biden Administration.

Israeli Prime Minister Benjamin Netanyahu has made it known that he believes it would be a "mistake" to go back to the Iran nuclear deal. In effect it would be providing them a secure period in which to develop the most easily delivered deadly weapons possible.

As readers of this series know, 2035 is the projected year when war will breakout in the Middle East and consume a major portion of Europe – with the United States drawn in as it has been in previous World Wars or European related conflicts. And, as stated, a nuclear war could produce a nuclear winter that would put an end to global warming and stabilize the planet.

It's not at all the solution most people would want.

While we hear about Climate Change and Global Warming, the fact that it tracks population growth is generally ignored. But if we look at the chart see that problem is one that really began with the Baby-Boom, and then only when the oldest of the Boomers was threatened with the Vietnam War. Then, the real issue of a rise in global temperatures seems to have been triggered when Reagan took office. Throughout the post-War Baby-boomer birth phase, global temoperatures were relatively flat and, when Reagan assumed office,

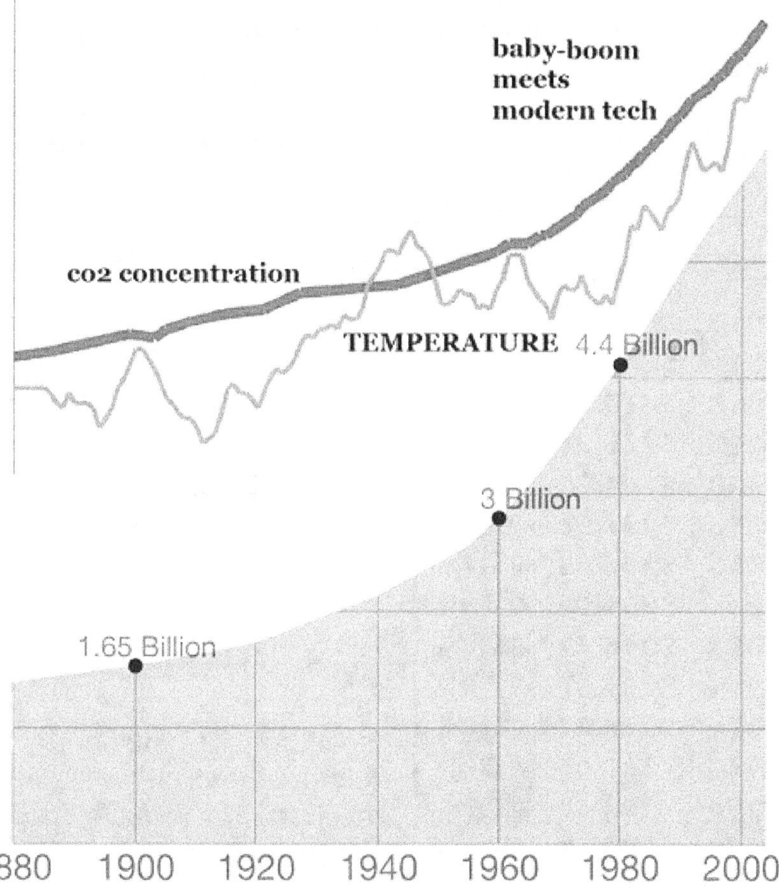

were no higher than they had been when FDR was elected.

As the chart shows, there was a sharp temperature rise during World War Two, a return to the levels in the late 1930s, and then another sharp rise during the Vietnam era of 1959-1963. Then, with Reagan, Bush, and Bush, we entered the period when modern tech met the adult Baby-boomers – but it was also the period when the Republicans promoted unending wars with the associated spikes in global temperatures. Even the spike leading into 1900 is a period when there was significant military action – for the United States, this would be marked by the Spanish-American War of April–August 1898. But it was actually a chain of British sponsored wars that had erupted throughout the end of the 19th century.

It is not the CO_2 concentration, but the human propensity to murder fellow humans, that has created and then perpetuated global warming.

As we go past the chart date of 2000 and move to the current 2021, the evidence of accelerated warming has increased. And, even though we do not recognize the effect, since 2001 there has been a wide scale combat situation – the United States Bush response to 9/11 saw both the murder of Saddam Hussein and the destabilization of the Middle East.

U.S. Military Spending/Defense Budget - Historical Data		
Year	US $Billions	Change
2015	$633.83	-2.16%
2014	$647.79	-4.63%
2013	$679.23	-6.34%
2012	$725.21	-3.60%
1998	$291.00	-0.74%
1996	$287.96	-2.67%
1995	$295.85	-3.97%
1994	$308.08	-2.73%
1993	$316.72	-2.56%
1991	$299.37	-7.92%
1971	$78.24	-6.20%
1970	$83.41	-1.86%
1964	$53.43	-2.07%
1963	$54.56	-0.16%

Bush initiated his 21-year war, thereby accelerating global warming through a roughly 15% increase in military spending for the 3-year period of 2002/03/04. As perverse as it seems, when the U.S. military budget increases so does warming.

As this table shows, since 1960, only 14-years have seen a decline in year-to-year military spending. Coincidently, global temperatures either stabilized or declined as the budget declined.

Trump's effort to withdraw

from the Bush initiated conflict and his apparently correct belief that there is no rational basis for the Paris Climate agreement – as seen with a 3 February court finding that France failed to respect its climate change goal – a failure made more dramatic, as pointed out by director of the Urgenda environmental group, Marjan Minnesma, who said of the ruling: "*Fantastic, because it is a big country and if you have the Paris accord to your name, then it's bizarre that you don't achieve your goals.*"

The court ruling placed a spotlight on the failure of all the signatories to meet their contractual responsibility. But, for the U.S., the problem of global warming might better be addressed by the nation reducing its military budget to a rational and less violently-aggressive level, while also pulling troops out of combat zones. There is no rational reason for the nation to play "Policeman to the World." And there certainly is no justification for America to use force in order to modify the internal politics of nations devoted to their own self-destruction.

If that self-destructive nation wishes to carry their poison into other nations, and invaded nation publically requests assistance from America in the form of forceful assistance, the answer is simply – use drones and maximum one-time force to erase the offending nation from the map.

However, because the warming has been locked in by global military actions, Greenland's ice sheet is melting seven times faster than it was in 1990 – which is more rapidly than the scientists had predicted. As a result, the 2019 sea-level rise prediction for 2100 is now 26.3 inches.

Just over two feet doesn't sound like much, but it means more than 400 million people will be at risk for destructive and costly flooding. Moreover, the combined warming and sea level rise will spawn mass migrations. In the United States, low-lying states like Florida can look forward to being underwater – since Washington DC was built on swamp land, it too faces submersion. The same would apply to the southern tip of Manhattan Island and any areas that are constructed on landfill.

Pay attention to the MSM. Have they even begun to raise the alarm? Do they even care that many parts of the country are going to be a modern version of Holland – which was constructed below sea level and were kept dry by dykes that held back the ocean, and windmills that pumped the water away.

While the politicians play with symbolic climate responses, to Americans South we have Mexico emerging as a major user of coal – thus placing itself in the position of becoming a major contributor to Climate Change.

In describing the Mexican Presidents motivation or method of achieving energy sovereignty, the director of Iniciativa Climática de México, Adrián Fernández Bremauntz, stated that, *"Instead of thinking of a transition from coal and fossil fuels, he's thinking of using more coal and petroleum. ... No other G20 country has such abnormal or retrograde energy policies as this government. ... It's not going to advance us toward our climate goals."*

Of course, MSM will remain quiet and Biden's Administration has no means of addressing the issue.

For now, executives like Jeremy Martin, vice-president for energy and sustainability at the Institute of the Americas, are saying *"The Paris agreement has zero relevance to anything they're talking about in the electric sector right now."*

What is happening in Mexico is being echoed in numerous other nations. And while automotive firms like Jaguar have made a clear commitment to following the Chinese model and producing only electric vehicles after 2025, until the United States commits to ending its commitment to centralized power defined by the grid, and moves to installing po9ihnt-of-use electric augmented by that grid, ther will be no real change in the progress of global warming.

Of course, MSM doesn't care. Their interest, like that of the politicians who belong to the Silent and early Boomer generations, are short term – how short was seen in the idea that we heard how vital it was to impeach a President who only had two weeks left to his term in office. And they knew their base was so stupid as to buy the idea, even though it was clear that there could be no trial until after his successor had been Inaugurated and in office for several weeks.

Remember, the important thing is always distract the gullible audience from wanting to know whatever is happening behind the curtain. And if someone comes along who wants to pull back the curtain, the Wizard will demand you attack them with everything you can and extol the virtue of NEVER believing a thing that is said. Those looking behind the curtain are always liars.

CHAPTER THREE – Covid-19

"If you have a vaccine, like the Moderna and the Pfizer vaccine, that can suppress the virus at a dilution, let's say, of 1 to 1,000, and the mutant influences it by bringing it down to maybe 1 to 800, or something like that, you're still well above the line of not being effective. So there's that 'cushion' that even though it's diminished somewhat, it still is effective." ~ Anthony Fauci MD on virus mutation

On 3 January President Donald Trump criticized the Centers for Disease Control and Prevention, accusing it of propagating "fake news" by exaggerating the number of COVID-19 cases and deaths in the United States. The number of United States COVID-19 cases had passed 20-million the death toll surpassed 350,000, by far the highest credited deaths in the world, followed by Brazil – reporting over 195,000 deaths. Trump tweeted that the numbers are inflated because of the CDC's "ridiculous method of determination compared to other countries."

Fauci responded in a manner that obscures the reality: *"The deaths are real deaths. I mean, all you need to do is to go out into the trenches, go to the hospitals, see what the health care workers are dealing with. They are under very stressed situations in many areas of the country, the hospital beds are stretched. People are running out of beds, running out of trained personnel who are exhaustive right now. That's real, that's not fake. Those are real numbers, real people and real deaths."*

But let's gain some perspective. Over 40% of the deaths are among the 1% residing in nursing homes. As covered earlier in this series, both New York Governor Andrew Cuomo and New York City Mayor Bill De Blasio made decisions which amplified this death toll. On his CNN show, the Governor's brother Chris Cuomo contributed to covering up the failures and blamed Trump for the problems.

But, with Trump out of office, CNN viewership declined and New York officials no longer had a scapegoat to hide behind. Biden was brought into office immune from MSM criticism – he was placed above the law.

With the spotlight off Trump, people are looking to New York and seeing a state where vaccines are spoiling in refrigerators while Cuomo's incompetence hampers distribution. Cuomo even nixed the city's plan to vaccinate 25,000 police officers – people whose duty it is to protect and serve weren't considered worth protecting.

Of course the pandemic is real, but Fauci has avoided the true reality of Covid as a culling virus rather than a 1918 flu style killing one. We can quickly see the difference in the CDC weekly report numbers.

In Book 11, I presented charts based on 5-week periods, in the last week of December, after the book went to press, the CDC revised all its numbers for 2019 and 2020. Those revisions are presented in the charts presented here. Only this time, I grouped the numbers as four week periods, calculated the difference between corresponding periods to establish what changed between the causes of death.

As the chart shows, as of 13 January 2021, there is a problem with the numbers. That problem is reflected in the fact that, when comparing 2019 with 2020, the number of excess deaths from ALL causes roughly does not match the reported deaths from Covid-19. We can account for some difference in the numbers due to the extra reporting period in 2020 (53 weeks rather than 52). But if we look at the chart, we see several normal causes of death are significantly negative. That is, fewer people are reported to have died because their deaths are attributed to Covid-19.

On 22 January 2021, the British GUARDIAN reported on an undercount of Covid-19 related fatalities. Under the UK system, if 28 days after testing positive, someone dies of complications result of Covid, they are not included in the quoted government figure. As we will show later in this chapter, U.S. policy is to attribute the cause of death to Covid-19 if the individual contracted – as the chart shows it doesn't matter if the person has a co-morbidity that, statistically, would have caused their death withing the same annual time frame.

There is a bigger issue.

Both Baby-Boomer and Silent generations have achieved or exceeded their average life expectancy; therefore, independent of a Covid-19 effect, the number of deaths would have been expected to increase significantly. The average life expectancy for males is 76.4 years. But the mathematics of the Baby-Bust is causing that number to raise – it is also noted that, statistically, women tend to outlive men by 4.8 years.

Still, the first of the Baby-Boom generation turned 70 in 2015 and the youngest members of the Silent Generation were turning 76 when the pandemic occurred.

The Baby-Boomer birth rate in 1946 was 24% higher than that of the Silent Generation and, by 1957, it had climbed to 54% higher – it held that level until 1961. This means the death rate will continue climb until 2034 – assuming that life expectancies remain within a range comparable to current global averages.

Since new children are not being added at replacement levels, increased longevity would ensure the population continues to grow until we enter the 2034 death cycle. At that point, the religious will point to the drop as a fulfillment of the Revelation prophecy calling for the death of a third of all life.

Climate Change extinctions that have already begun will serve to ensure statistical changes conform to the prediction. Since past warming cycles have generally been accompanied by various species dying off, oral tradition and observation at the time the prophecy was rendered would be sufficient to explain its accuracy.

Since Covid-19 is actually a culling virus, the anticipated rise is lost in the reporting. However it does show in the CDC differences between 2019 and 2020 – as shown on the chart of weekly data as it

As of 13 January Coronavirus related death: 408,491	ANNUAL	Totals: POSITIVE NEGATIVE DIFFERENCE
All Cause 2020-2019	**365,581**	
Natural Cause 2020-2019	**878,741**	
Septicemia (A40-A41)	(128,117)	
Malignant neoplasms (C00-C97)	102,310	300,157
Diabetes mellitus (E10-E14)	494	
Alzheimer disease (G30)	23,207	
Influenza and pneumonia (J09-J18)	(24,610)	
Chronic lower respiratory diseases (J40-J47)	16,552	(263,656)
Other diseases of respiratory system	(2,471)	
Nephritis, nephrotic syndrome and nephrosis	3,607	
Symptoms, signs and abnormal clinical and laboratory findings, not elsewhere classified	(108,458)	
Diseases of heart (I00-I09,I11,I13,I20-I51)	117,198	36,501
Cerebrovascular diseases (I60-I69)	36,789	
COVID-19 (U071, Multiple Cause)	**277,750**	**Covid related deaths**
COVID-19 (U071, Underlying Cause)	**252,318**	

was reported on 6 January 2021 as revised on 13 January.

By 18 January, the reported death toll had reached 408,491. As we see on the chart, the difference in deaths from all causes for 2019 and 2020 was 365,581 – the difference is roughly consistent with the weekly deaths attributed to Covid-19.

But note something strange on the chart. Of the eleven most common medical causes of death, four of which – totaling 263,656 – had gone negative. That is, when reporting the cause of death, Covid-19 had replaced the traditional cause of death. This is then covered by "co-morbidity" classifications without a clear statement that, absent the pandemic, individuals would have died anyway.

If we take note of the negatives in the last few periods of the

year, we see a significant number of negative values – these indicate that those who would have died at the end of the year passed earlier.

Therefore the increased number of deaths for 2020 are best seen as the combined effect of a culling of those who would have died 2021 plus the Baby-Boomers reaching their natural expiration date and a few surviving Silent Generation members. This is supported by the reports dating back to October when the CDC reported that about 8 in 10 Covid-19 deaths were among those who were 65 and older.

In December, the CDC reported that those under the age of 34 accounted for less than 1% of total deaths; those 35 to 44 accounted for 1.88% of deaths; those over the age of 54 accounted for 97.18 percent of total Covid deaths.

If we look at racial minorities, we discover 78% of COVID-19 deaths under the age of 21 were in minority communities; January 2021 saw research papers that attributed those deaths to skin color – specifically the effect of high levels of Melanin, which causes skin pigmentation, and lowers the body's ability to make Vitamin D. This then causes a Vitamin D deficiency which weakens the body's ability to resist the effects of Covid-19.

If Africa and other high sun region, the darker skin serves to protect the body and still produce sufficient levels of Vitamin D. But in higher latitudes and within the modern Office or factory cultures, the lack of sunshine triggers the deficiency.

This immune system connection is actually a relatively new

discovery. The relationship between Vitamin D and strong bones has been well established. During the Second World War, Winston Churchill's people were concerned with people developing rickets, a musculoskeletal condition; in order *"to safeguard the nutritional status of the nation"* they issued orders for margarine companies to fortify their products with vitamin D – this continued until 2013, when it was deemed unnecessary.

It will be interesting to see if researches discover that the high rate of Covid-19 in the U.K. is, in part, due to a general Vitamin D3 deficiency associated with the discontinuing of that wartime order.

As stated in a letter from the British Association of Physicians of Indian Origin, *"People born with darker skin receive less UV light in the deeper layers where D3 is made, and so are prone to more severe D-deficiency at the end of winter in northern latitudes than their fairer-skinned counterparts."*

The table/chart shows the CDC weekly deaths restructured into quarters and reduced to the difference between 2020 and 2019. The bottom two lines are Covid-19 related, while the top two are deaths from all causes {Line 1} and deaths from natural causes {Line 2}. However it is the middle eleven categories that are significant – notice that the fourth quarter comparison shows that eight of them went negative when 2019 was subtracted from 2020.

Now turn your attention to the summation chart on the next page, where we see four of the eleven categories are negative on a year-over-year basis. Unless the medical issues were eliminated, that result would be impossible to achieve in an aging population.

However, Dr. Brix and President Trump told us this would be the case. In April 2020, Dr. Deborah Birx stated: "If Someone Dies With COVID-19 We Are Counting That As A COVID-19 Death." And at a Wisconsin rally in October, Trump told his audience: "*You know some countries they report differently. If somebody's sick with a heart problem, and they die of COVID they say they die of a heart problem. If somebody's terminally ill with cancer and they have COVID, we report them. And you know doctors get more money and hospitals get more money. Think of this incentive.*"

In January 2021, Trump Tweeted: "*The number of cases and deaths of the China Virus is far exaggerated in the United States because of the @CDCgov's ridiculous method of determination compared to other countries, many of whom report, purposely, very inaccurately and low."*

Since February 2020 the MSM has scoffed at Trump claims of problems with the reporting on Covid-19 and that, within a short time, it would "disappear."

But the media continues to report cases – the overwhelming majority of which are asymptomatic and in fact are discovered only because of widespread testing.

The method of counting deaths used by the CDC, as stated by Dr. Brix, classifies any death from a comorbidity as Covid if the patient contracted Covid-19. The negative numbers the illustration emphasize the effect of that policy – four categories are a negative 263,656, or about two-thirds of the Covid-19 deaths.

Consider Septicemia a serious bloodstream infection which most people know as "Blood poisoning." Were there really 128,117 fewer cases in 2020 than 2019? And what about other common things like Influenza and Pneumonia – did they suddenly vanish and result in 24,610 fewer cases?

Covid-19 is a Culling Virus. It attacks those who have either recognized or unrecognized medical conditions.

On 19 January, one day before Joe Biden became President, the United States reported 24,655,637 cases; of those 14,557,409 recovered and 409,029 died. That means, roughly 7-percent of all Americans were identified as having Covid-19; of that 7-percent, 60-percent recovered, and 1.6-percent died – the rest are either new cases or undergoing treatment.

Among 'long Covid' suffers – those whose symptoms seem to wander through their bodies – there is a sustained inability to return to work; others who have "recovered" have shown evidence of patterns of neurologic damage or sustained cognitive impairment.

A third of those suffering Covid-19 related respiratory failure have also evidenced a loss of the brain's executive function, resulting in difficulties understanding the written word and communicating verbally, which is then accompanied by an inability to track daily responsibilities. This pattern of disruption in routine behavior can be equated to the normal behavior seen in President Biden's verbal gaffes – which existed without exposure to Covid-19.

Studies conducted prior to the inauguration show that many of those who recover from the virus suffer significant brain decline, and in worst case scenarios the effect equates to a ten year aging of the brain.

What the new studies reveal is that even when the virus does not cull those who are already seriously damage, low level damage can be amplified among survivors of hospitalization level effects. As of January 2021, there do not appear to be any studies indicating damage to those who are asymptomatic carriers.

What this means is that, while the virus is a culling one, those who are healthy should take the vaccine as a precaution against the further spread of the virus. It also means we need a much better heath care network – one that can detect hidden problems Covid-19 is exposing.

These problems can be severe medical issues underlying the death of younger members of the population, or simply vitamin deficiencies, such as with Vitamin D3 which the immune system needs to be fully functional.

Whether you are older or younger, if you contract Covid-19, and are not asymptomatic, it is likely you have a medical issue that would have in other ways. Of course, if you are over 55, contracting Covid-19 could result in death due to the pre-existing issues.

The difference in annual deaths was roughly the number of Covid deaths at the end of December. And while it is higher than the deaths in 2019, the number is not out of line with the anticipated number of deaths – a number that will rise every year until about 2040, when the remaining Silent generation and bulk of the Boomer generation have died. That will also be the year when the first of the Gen-X will be about 75-years-old.

The upside to the pandemic was revealed on 28 January, when more than 50 progressive Democrats urged President Biden to consider recurring stimulus checks – effectively a practical test of UBI that echos the pandemic response in other major nations.

Ideally these checks would be about $2,000 a month – This amounts to $24,000 per year, which is above poverty and would, if made permanent, actually save the government money relative to the cost of Public Assistance costs. Public Assistance for citizens could cease to exist.

Based on the Census Bureau's 2016 Annual Surveys of State and Local Government Finances, the total public welfare spending – including Old Age Assistance, Temporary Assistance for Needy

Families – exceeded $637 billion. By 2020, that number exceeded $1 trillion. If we add to that cost the effective expenditure associated with the personal deduction on taxes the amount is even higher; it goes even higher if we include unemployment insurance.

We can play with the number and get whatever we want as an argument. But the reality is, the government is spending the money and spending more during a pandemic or economic downturn – all of which goes away with UBI, which can be delivered by Debt Card.

In fact, it should be a direct bank deposit where the account provides the debt card – which would ensure that only citizens or legal residents receive the funds. Those who wish to increase the bureaucratic involvement and cost to government associated with welfare and related programs will oppose it. But those seeking to grow the economy will promote it.

If you wish a slave economy, you add bureaucratic structure that requires people to "prove" they are destitute. They are reduced to beggars trying to convince the servants of the provincial Lord that they need assistance – which the servants are hired to deny.

People will still work, because work will add to the money they receive. But even if they do not work, the income will still be spent and serve as a stable foundation to both the local and national economy.

CHAPTER FOUR – Impeach

"I know that everyone here will soon be marching over to the Capitol building to peacefully and patriotically make your voices heard." ~DJT, 6 January 2021

After the Electoral College Vote was confirmed, and the rioter stormed the Capital – stealing a laptop from Pelosi – it appeared Pelosi and Schumer agreed they wanted to secure Trump's place in the history books.

On 7 January the Swamp Denizens began screaming for both Impeachment and implementation of 25th Amendment. They did not care which was applied to highlight the final days of the Trump Administration, so long as it was historically noteworthy.

With the 25th Amendment, Trump would be declared unfit to carry out his Presidential responsibilities and Vice President Mike Pence would become acting President for the last few days of their Administration.

Since Pence refused to yield or bow to Pelosi's will, it became necessary for her to seek passage of a resolution formally calling on Vice President Mike Pence to invoke it and strip President Trump of his duties by declaring Trump *"incapable of executing the duties of his office and to immediately exercise powers as acting president."*

Of course, the Impeachment would require that the House set a record for both writing and passing Articles of Impeachment – of course, given the timeframe, the new House managers would not be burdened with inventing some quasi-valid basis for impeachment. With less than two weeks until the inauguration, Pelosi was free to implement any fraudulent justification she desired.

There was no need for the Senate to accept it, or even debate it. The Articles of Impeachment were said to reach the Senate floor on the 19th or soon after the 20th – at which point the whole matter would be moot because President Biden would be in the Oval Office.

However, as the inauguration approached, Pelosi repeated what she had done with the first set of Articles and simply held on to the new set – the anticipated date they would be delivered to the Senate was now after the 25th.

Pelosi and Schumer found no problem in wasting public time and money – anything they can do to delay the Biden agenda serves their goals. It doesn't matter that they are the same party, harming the people is the only thing they are devoted to.

Biden realized the reality and immediately upon being sworn in began the process of issuing Executive Orders – 17 on the day he was sworn in. His objective was clear – get anything that doesn't require Congressional action done immediately. He wasn't about to echo Pelosi and procrastinate in doing the People's Business. In the meantime, Pelosi, who had managed to pass a second set of Articles of Impeachment in a matter of hours – without the need for either evidence or witnesses – was now saying the promised $2,000, that had been reduced to $1,400, would not even be introduced before the first week in February.

Republican Senator Roy Blunt that the legislation would have problematic items included and therefore told reporters: "*I suspect the whole package is a non-starter, but it's got plenty of starters in it.*"

Since many Americans do not understand what Impeachment is, they do not understand why it became moot on 21 January. Still, California's Democratic Senator Dianne Feinstein had no problem explaining to reporters: "*I think it's a moot question. This president is leaving office so it won't have any practical application. But whatever happens is fine with me.*"

In terms of priorities, Connecticut Democratic Senator Chris Murphy voiced the opinion: "*My clear preference is to create room for nominations and legislation. I'll defer to leadership but I don't know that we have to start the trial right after the inauguration.*"

And West Virginia's Democratic Senator Joe Manchin said of the impeachment, it "*doesn't make any common sense whatsoever.*"

However, the consistently dishonest Schumer stated, "*There will be an impeachment trial in the United States Senate. There will be a vote on convicting the president for high crimes and misdemeanors. And if the president is convicted, there will be a vote on barring him from running again.*"

Some might as where the dishonesty is, but they ignore the fact that the Articles were passed without any factual basis in the form of evidence, witnesses, or legal expert opinion on whether one can impeach – seek to remove – a "former" President, a person who has already been legally removed from office.

On 20 January, Joni Ernst, a Republican Senator from Iowa,

expressed the opinion that Schumer and Pelosi were promoting an unconstitutional action stating, "*I've read arguments on both sides but he's not our president after tomorrow so the only reason I can see is that Democrats want to further divide the nation and [I'm] asking President-elect Joe Biden, 'Please, let's move forward.'*"

Meanwhile, Kirsten Gillibrand, a Democratic Senator from New York held that a trial based on charges without either witnesses or evidence meant "*We could conduct a trial in a very, relatively, short time.*" That is, because he was charged, he is guilty – Guilty until proved innocent, and there would be no evidence or witnesses allowed who could assert that innocence because "*This article of impeachment is nothing like the previous articles of impeachment, which were highly complex, relied on multiple witnesses, multiple documents.*"

Let's do a quick review of Article II, Section 4 which states, "*The President, Vice President and all civil Officers of the United States, **shall be removed from Office** on Impeachment for, and Conviction of, Treason, Bribery, or other high Crimes and Misdemeanors.*"

Note the critical words that serve as the goal or penalty, the objective is that they "***shall be removed from Office.***" But, on 20 January Trump's term ends and Biden's begins – at that point, when Biden is sworn in, Donald John Trump would be legally and officially removed from office. The impeachment thus becomes an exercise in stupidity, futility, or an intentional political ploy aimed at allowing Pelosi and Schumer to avoid taking any legislative action to introduce and have ready the Biden Agenda.

The comedy is, House Democrats wrote a lengthy report to accompany their article of impeachment which acknowledged, "*The president's remaining term is limited — but a president capable of fomenting a violent insurrection in the Capitol is capable of greater dangers still. He must be removed from office as swiftly as the Constitution allows. He must also be disqualified to prevent the recurrence of the extraordinary threat he presents.*"

But, we need to ask, does the Constitution allow the removal of a POTUS who has been lawfully removed by an election?

The answer is basic – and, apparently, NO!

Within days of Biden's inauguration, ex-U.S. Court of Appeals Judge J. Michael Luttig voiced the legal opinion that, "*Once Trump's term ends on January 20, Congress loses its constitutional authority to continue impeachment proceedings against him – even if the House has already approved articles of impeachment."*

Citing Article 1, Section 3, and Article II, Section 4, Luttig stated, *"The reason for this is found in the Constitution itself. Trump would no longer be an incumbent in the office of the President at the time of the delayed Senate proceeding, and would no longer be subject to 'impeachment conviction' by the Senate, under the Constitution's Impeachment Clauses. Which is to say that the Senate's only power under the Constitution is to convict – or not – an incumbent president."*

Harvard Law professor and Democrat Alan Dershowitz fully concurred and added, *"… the Constitution specifically says, 'The President shall be removed from office upon impeachment.' It doesn't say the former president. Congress has no power to impeach or try a private citizen, whether it be a private citizen named Donald Trump or named Barack Obama, or anyone else. The jurisdiction is limited to a sitting president, and so there won't be a trial."*

In this case, Trump's people were questioning whether or not the election was lawful. And many witness assertions indicate there is probable to believe the final vote count is wrong.

As for the idea Trump sponsored sedition, Representative Matt Gaetz of Florida, placed that idea in context, alleging *"the Left in America has incited far more political violence than the Right."* An allegation which has ample supporting documentation, while there is also documentation that Trump instructed his followers to behave in a "Peaceful" manner. Then, there was also the timeline of events – the infiltration of the Capitol occurred early in Trump's one hour speech, at a time when the people he was address were roughly two miles away.

Did the Founding Fathers intend impeachment to be a post-election, post-transition, vindictive tool for a deceptive dictatorial element that is fearful the voters will see through their deception?

"Sedition" is a cute term. When used by the House leadership it is also a deceptive lie consistent with California's entertainment culture. In mid-July 2020, vandalism at Trump Tower was greeted with Mayor De Blasio aiding the vandals in creating a mural on the street in front of the landmark building.

In the same time period, Tucker Carlson asserted that "Black Lives Matter" [BLM] protests represented a "hysteria" pandemic because it spreads much like Covid-19. As Carlson stated, "*We now know that the craziness spreads very much the same way, and we're now living through a pandemic of it.*"

In February, both De Blasio and Pelosi reacted to Covid-19 by encouraging superspreader behavior. When the BLM rampage and destruction showed its concern for minorities by looting or burning minority community businesses, Pelosi and De Blasio dismissed the behavior as "peaceful demonstrations" to be encouraged or excused.

For Trump, the nonsensical political act only underscores the reality the world has witnessed for four years – beginning when the election results were announced in November 2016. The current Democratic leadership are petty children with limited IQ's who have been fortunate enough to have an electorate that is even dumber and more petty than they are.

For Trump, securing a noteworthy place in history has always been a driving force behind his actions. Pelosi and her minions are seeking to obediently serve that objective.

In this instance, the goal is to make Donald John Trump the only President in American history to be impeached twice – and that action occurred his only term in office. Moreover, he ended or lost re-election with the largest vote ever attained by an incumbent – while he was defeated by the largest vote in history, meaning Biden enters office with an historic burden to justify.

As the victory tally was reported by USA Today:

"Biden won 81 million votes and 509 counties in the Nov. 3 election, while Trump won 74 million votes and 2,547 counties, according to data aggregated by think tank the Brookings Institute. Obama won 69 million votes and 873 counties in 2008. But that doesn't mean the election was fraudulent."

Clearly, social media played the same strong role it did when Hillary was running. And, as we know, Biden didn't have people showing at rallies – so they did not vote for him, rather they were doing what the MSM told them to do – voting against Trump.

Historians would have a field day.

Since any valid historical analysis generally occurs a decade or more after the event, the historians would be writing with full knowledge of the Harris-Biden Administration ability to function in face of a Congress under the leadership of Nancy Pelosi and Chuck Schumer.

The fact that a 31-year-old Alexandria Ocasio-Cortez (AOC) had indicated she was seriously contemplating running against her fellow New York Democrat, and now Senate Majority Leader – the 70-year-old Charles Ellis Schumer – was sufficient evidence that he had become an incompetent Baby-Boomer dinosaur the Progressive left wanted to see gone from a position of Senatorial power.

It will be a decade or more before the blatant dishonesty that has been the hallmark of Pelosi and Schumer practices would come to light – first they must be removed from power, and then it may be legally or politically necessary to await their deaths.

One thing of note is that, after the 6 January riot, FaceBook locked the Trump account – ever since she graduated Harvard, Schumer's youngest daughter, Alison, has been part of FaceBook's management and serves as a marketing manager in the company's New York office. That political connection would ensure FaceBook would do everything it could to justify silencing Schumer's political targets.

After all, it is, effectively, the same game Hunter Biden has profited from. As the Wall Street Journal phrased it, *"Hunter Biden ramped up business activities with European and Chinese tycoons as his father exited the vice presidency four years ago. For him it was a potential path to income; for the tycoons, the Biden family name promised to burnish their reputations."*

As cited in Book-08 of the Trump card series:

"John Solomon reported: 'Just three weeks before Burisma's overture to State, Ukrainian authorities raided the home of the oligarch who owned the gas firm and employed Hunter Biden, a signal the long-running corruption probe was escalating in the middle of the U.S. presidential election. Hunter Biden's name, in fact, was specifically invoked by the Burisma representative as a reason the State Department should help, according to a series of email exchanges among U.S. officials trying to arrange the meeting.'"

Biden has his leverage, and Schumer clearly exerts leverage within the realm of Social Media. Having exerted that power in their effort to silence Trump, Pelosi and Schumer decided that – since

Trump can be deemed too dangerous for his social media accounts, it follows that he must be too dangerous to remain in charge of the executive branch, the military, and nuclear launch codes.

With regard to the latter, their Social media agents were then called upon to immediately declare that Trump's last act as POTUS would be to initiate a war with Iran.

Given their desire to undermine American Democracy, it followed that Pelosi would declare: *"We are in a very dangerous place in this country as long as Donald Trump remains in office. While it is only 13 days left, any day can be a horror show for America."*

Hopefully, the nation can survive until 2022, when both Schumer and Pelosi can be voted out and replaced with rational and responsible Democratic leadership. There would also be the need to replace the remaining Swamp Denizens like Illinois Representative Adam Kinzinger or any who have aligned with the Lincoln Project.

The horrors and incompetence of the 116th Congress came to an end and, on 3 January, the 117th Congress convened to initiate a repeat of the stupidity and misrepresentation exhibited by most of them as they served as their own predecessors.

We can rest assured that there shall never be a proper audit of the 2020 election. We know the Swamp shouted Russian fraud when Trump won in 2016; now that Trump has asserted a repeat of that fraud, the Swamp Denizens are dismissing the idea.

In 2016, it was pointed out that Russians used Social media to reach their intended targets. However, since Social Media only dominates areas won by Hillary Clinton, and the propagandists did not take into account the Electoral College, Clinton was denied the victory that would have come if the elections were controlled by major population centers.

In 2020, things were modified to target the major population regions within low population states – the propagandists seemed to have learned their lesson and they achieve a Biden victory.

However, we see the same problem we saw in 2016.

While Biden won the popular vote – just as Hillary had done four years earlier – his total victory majority could be accounted for by the majority carried in Southern California and New York City. That is, the same propaganda foundation established in 2016 was in place and working in 2020. Going forward, the only issue will be the way it is improved upon for the 2024 election cycle.

Should a non-POTUS Cousin come to power in 2024 or if we see Harris replace Biden before 2024, we can be assured that the United States has been overthrown and the leadership history that began with the first Colonial Leadership over 400-years ago finally has ended.

It would be possible to have – as with Donald John Trump or Andrew Jackson – a descent of the 4-Sisters who is not themselves a POTUS Cousin, but is related to one through marriage.

If that were to happen, then the nation would once again be treated to a tumultuous experience of the type that marked both the Jackson and Trump eras. Whoever that POTUS might be, they can be assured that, as with Jackson and Trump, their place in history and timelessly persistent public recognition shall be assured.

However, as of this writing, we need only concern ourselves with the actions of the 117th Congress – will it approve the $2,000 survival stimulus check; will it see Covid-19 as a culling virus that was predicted 2,000-years ago as part of the forces, combined with Climate Change, that are destined to reduce all life by a third before the year 2050?

Shall both POTUS Biden and the 117th Congress join forces and secure America's place as a self-sufficient mercantile nation that is on a level footing as China returns to his traditional mercantile role in global commerce? Or, will America move to become even more dependent upon China for basics like medicine and technology that will define the post-apocalyptic era?

People on both sides of the aisle need to awaken and realize that 2016 – the year that gave us BREXIT and Trump – was also the hottest year on record. As of the close of 2020, humanity has seen the hottest decade ever recorded globally.

The Arctic has experienced extreme heat and atmospheric concentrations of planet-warming carbon dioxide continued to rise, even as the pandemic has reduced the use of fossil fuels to a greater extent than was called for in the Paris Climate Accord.

Then there is the observed paradox of the same greenhouse gases cooling the upper atmosphere even as the lower atmosphere grows warmer. As the climate warms people react through a shift in their migration patterns – as noted earlier, this has been the reality of human evolution and cultural advancement throughout the past.

Part of the evolutionary process is a change in government or forms of leadership. Originally, people were tribal, then the tribes unified, as described in the Biblical creation of Israel by Moses, and the leadership of the wisest or unifying tribe assumed that role over many tribes. There was, of course, conflict – people died. That death can be via either war or disease, though it is, as Revelation has described it would be, generally a combination of both.

We have seen the first stages in the 2020 election, the calls for impeachment, the violence, and the general discord that has split the polulation and political parties.

It's not just America, we see it in the European Union and the United Kingdom's BREXIT. The peace treaties between Israel and its Arab neighbors are the first signs of a forming unification that is a necessity before that region enters into a final war.

Interestingly, "*despite a 7% fall in fossil fuel burning due to coronavirus lockdowns, heat-trapping carbon dioxide continued to build up in the atmosphere, also setting a new record.*" That noted build-up was accompanied by some of the cleanest air since the start of the Industrial Revolution. Still, the average surface temperature of the planet came within a quarter degree Celsius of the temperature that would trigger the worst impact on nature as we know it.

Looking ahead, optimistically, we have until 2050 to halt the process.

Or, as phrased by the UK's MET Office Prof Richard Betts:

"The human-caused buildup of CO2 in the atmosphere is accelerating. It took over 200 years for levels to increase by 25%, but now just over 30 years later we are approaching a 50% increase. Global emissions will need to be brought down to net zero within about the next 30 years if global warming is to be limited to 1.5C."

Climate Change is one of the many things Schumer and Pelosi want to avoid dealing with – hence we saw then promote what was a meaningless impeachment.

Since Pelosi was unable to blackmail Vice President Michael Pence into turning against President Donald Trump – by invoking the 25th Amendment – she went forward with the meaningless 2nd attempt to impeach, knowing full well that she could not remove a president who has already been removed by the Electoral College.

As with most fascist impersonators, Pelosi invoked the big lie by claiming a legitimate basis that existed only in the rhetoric: *"In protecting our Constitution and our Democracy, we will act with urgency, because this President represents an imminent threat to both. As the days go by, the horror of the ongoing assault on our democracy perpetrated by this President is intensified and so is the immediate need for action."*

Pelosi was not protecting the Constitution. As we saw in the quote, Article II, Section 4 deals with removal for actions which should prohibit the accused from holding any further governmental positions of trust.

But Trump has been removed, and that removal was, by law, set for the 20th of January 2021.

Supposedly, it is a crime to claim you won an election. Or, as Pelosi's written statement phrased it, *"There, he reiterated false claims that 'we won this election, and we won it by a landslide.' He also willfully made statements that encouraged — and foreseeably resulted in — imminent lawless action at the Capitol."*

Curiously, by every metric relevant to the past 150 years of election results indicated, Trump should have been the winner. He won four times more counties, won the bell-weather states, and set a record for votes received by an incumbent.

Obviously, the remaining GOP Swamp Denizens would jump in line behind any effort to disgrace or undermine Trump and the Constitution. Accordingly, 17 or the need 18 Republicans jumped at the chance to promote Pelosi's agenda.

There is a "conspiracy" question assoc9iated with the lawless behavior. The Trump rally was a scheduled event. That means there was ample time for D.C. police to follow customary protocol for a large gathering and increase available manpower. But they did not do that.

On 11 January, the Associated Press reported, *"CAPITOL POLICE WERE 'LEFT NAKED' Despite ample warnings ..."* Apparently the Capitol Police did not increase their staffing to address the normal rally safeguards. As a result, when the crowd began to move toward the Capital, there were insufficient officers for proper crowd control. Moreover, videos show the police opening the crowd control fences to let the protesters through.

The AP article revealed that Capitol Police Chief Steven Sund, who resigned soon after the event, saw to it that *"the same number of officers in place as on a routine day."* And when a request was made for deployment of the waiting National Guard reinforcements, there were hours of bureaucratic problems and concerns about the optics of troops outside the Capitol. Instead, the optics showed Senators and House members cowering behind desks with the doors blocked and security officers with guns drawn ready to slaughter the protesters.

Slowly and very briefly, other MSM outlets became to report that, days or weeks before the event, the FBI had been aware of the planned violence and had even approached the extremists to warn them against attending the rally.

We also have Trump's words from the rally, words Pelosi and Schumer say incited extremist action that the FBI was already aware of and supposedly addressing:

"We have come to demand that Congress do the right thing and only count the electors who have been lawfully slated, lawfully slated. I know that everyone here will soon be marching over to the Capitol building to peacefully and patriotically make your voices heard. Today we will see whether Republicans stand strong for integrity of our elections, but whether or not they stand strong for our country, our country."

Republican Representative Matt Gaetz of Florida, attacked the 2nd Impeachment, and joined numerous others in pointing out that *"the Left in America has incited far more political violence than the Right."*

In support of his assertion, on 15 January the MSM reported that *"Antifa supporter Daniel Alan Baker was just arrested for plotting an attack on Trump supporters on Inauguration Day."* And this attack on TRUMP SUPPORTERS – not the Democrats – included a New Yorker who had traveled to Washington to commit murder. That man, Dominic "Spaz" Pezzola, was allegedly captured on video smoking a cigar and saying words to the effect of, *"Victory smoke in the Capitol, boys. This is fucking awesome. I knew we could take this motherfucker over [if we] just tried hard enough."*

Pezzola's boastful assertion had nothing to do with anything Trump had said. It certainly was not related to the speech, since the culprit had traveled to Washington specifically to go on a bipartisan murder spree and he boasted he "*would have killed anyone they got their hands on, including Speaker of the House Nancy Pelosi and Vice President Michael Pence.*"

The response of Democratic leaders like Pelosi to the Antifa and BLM violence showed that they condoned burning and killing. Pezzola's intended actions were therefore spawned by the approval asserted in a meme posted to Facebook. The post read, "*Not a single Democrat has condemned nor called for an end of the BLM and ANTIFA caused violence. They are aiding and abetting mass violence across the country.*"

While the meme comment was not exactly accurate, fact checkers have pointed out that, on 31 May, Vice President Joe Biden "*wrote in a statement that protesting police brutality is 'right and necessary' and the 'American response.'*" Therefore we have Biden seeming to approve of the actions while adding the codicil, "*But burning down communities and needless destruction is not. Violence that endangers lives is not. Violence that guts and shutters businesses that serve the community is not.*"

On 30 August it was reported that Pelosi finally came around to condemning the actions – but only when they occurred in her own backyard – and she said: "*The violent actions of people calling themselves antifa in Berkeley this weekend deserve unequivocal condemnation, and the perpetrators should be arrested and prosecuted.*"

However, when a cancel culture mob pushed a Christopher Columbus into statue into Baltimore's Inner Harbor, Pelosi stated: "*If the community doesn't want the statue there, the statue shouldn't be there. ... I think that it's very important that we take down any of the statues of people who committed treason against the United States of America.*"

However, when asked if it wouldn't be more appropriate for an appointed commission to decide if any given status should be removed – rather than have a mob of vandals making the decision – Pelosi said: "*People will do what they do. I do think that from a safety standpoint, it would be a good idea to have it taken down if the community doesn't want it. I don't know that it has to be a commission.*"

In September 2020, the woman who became the nation's first

female Vice President, Senator Kamala Harris, stated: "*Nothing that we have achieved that has been about progress, in particular around civil rights, has come without a fight, and so I always am going to interpret these protests as an essential component of evolution in our country – as an essential component or mark of a real democracy.*"

Having said that, it would follow that protests to ensure the key component of democracy – a free and fair election in which all the votes are properly accounted for – would certainly demand there be protests.

When it came to the BLM protests, Harris made it clear that there were distinctions to be made, saying: "*We must always defend peaceful protest and peaceful protesters. We should not confuse them with those looting and committing acts of violence, including the shooter who was arrested for murder. Make no mistake, we will not let these vigilantes and extremists derail the path to justice.*"

Yet, in January 2021, the path of justice and adherence to the constitution was derailed when citizens peacefully protested what was an unexplained outcome to an election where the President was able to cite numerous instances of "discrepancies" – the transcript of the 6 January speech in which these are enumerated serves as the final chapter in the book. It was Trump and others challenging the specifics that are now being used as the basis for what is an unlawful impeachment – an act to remove a POTUS who is no longer POTUS.

Mitch McConnell cited the fact that there had only been three previous impeachments and that they lasted 83 days, 37 days, and 21 days. Pelosi had therefore decided to engage in two violations of her oath of office – she knowingly violated the Constitution and took engaged in an action intended to disrupt the Senate legislative process by anything from three to twelve weeks. She was willfully and knowingly attempting undermining implementation of Biden's Presidential agenda for his first hundred days (fourteen weeks).

Pelosi and Schumer seem to object to citizens seeking proof of a far and proper election expressing themselves "*peacefully and patriotically.*" They object to such a degree that they would willing violate the Constitution and their oath of office, while disrupting the legislative process to impede the ability of the newly elected POTUS to function during his first 100 days.

It is interesting that the MSM, Pelosi, Schumer, and others actively violating the Constitution declared BLM looters and vandals to be '*peaceful protesters*' as they set minority communities on fire, chose to define the rally as a mob engaged in a riot.

Speaking of Chief Sund's handling of the events, California Representative Maxine Waters stated: "*He kept assuring me he had it under control — they knew what they were doing. Either he's incompetent, or he was lying or he was complicit.*" However, this is the same Maxine Waters who, in November 2016, prepared the 1st Articles of Impeachment weeks before Trump's Inauguration. Then 6 January served as an excuse to promote what she had wanted for four years. Along with Nancy Pelosi, Waters continued her anti-American activities in the form of a meaningless political gesture.

While the 2nd Impeachment clearly violates the intention of the Founding Fathers and the purpose as stated in the Constitution, it does reveal the extent to which Pelosi and other Swamp Denizens feared Donald John Trump's efforts to "Drain the Swamp."

While Impeachment was intended to remove any who proved themselves to be a criminal or habitual violator of the Constitution from government, it carried with it a prohibition against any future service. As such, Pelosi was attempting to turn it into a political tool that would eliminate opposition candidates prior to future elections.

If Pelosi was successful, and if Schumer was able to convince the Senate to convict Trump on the bogus allegations, Trump would be prohibited from running in 2024 – meaning Biden would be free to be as incompetent, dishonest, and racist as past behavior showed he was. There would be no chance of voters exercising what could be termed either "Seller's or Buyer's Remorse." The prevailing fear was that they would realize that, for 4 years, they had been conned and they would retaliate by making Trump the 2nd President to be elected to two separate terms as POTUS 45 & 47 – Grover Cleveland (POTUS 22 & 24) being, to date, the first and only one.

However, Pelosi's success is that of a political manipulator and not a representative of the people.

On 11 January, Congresswoman Lauren Boebert denounced the Pelosi cabal and her Hollywood support for their hypocrisy. As she phrased it:

"We should take Democrats at their word when they say never let a crisis go to waste. Their hypocrisy is on full display with

talks of impeachment, censure, and other ways to punish Republicans for false accusations of inciting the type of violence they have so frequently and transparently supported in the past.

"And, once again, their false attacks go unchallenged. They accuse me of live-tweeting the Speaker's presence after she had been safely removed from the Capitol, as if I was revealing some big secret, when in fact this removal was also being broadcast on TV.

"They act as if Republicans created objections to the Electoral College certification out of thin air, when it was Democrats who objected in 2001, 2005 and 2017.

"The reality is that Joe Biden didn't condemn Antifa when he had a chance to, Kamala Harris spent much of the summer helping those arrested for violent behavior post bail and get back on the streets as quickly as possible, and Speaker Pelosi encouraged uprisings all over the country.

"But let's get real—the far-left and their policies are causing harm to our country. I refuse to let their political machine write a narrative that millions of Americans know is false."

And there is the point that will defeat Pelosi and Schumer – over 70 million voters recognize the false narrative, and nearly 80 million more will come to understand the reality – the will come to realize the Emperor has no clothes.

What is this Sedition?

The federal law against seditious conspiracy can be found in Title 18 of the U.S. Code (which includes treason, rebellion, and similar offenses), specifically 18 U.S.C. § 2384.

According to the statutory definition of sedition, it is a crime for two or more people within the jurisdiction of the United States: *"To conspire to overthrow or destroy by force the government of the United States or to level war against them; To oppose by force the authority of the United States government; to prevent, hinder, or delay by force the execution of any law of the United States; or To take, seize, or possess by force any property of the United States contrary to the authority thereof."*

Pelosi is acting to prevent Biden from initiating his agenda and to delay or block the Senate vote on his Cabinet appointments.

She has already taken possession of the House of Representatatives.

A driving force behind the realization will be experts such as Democratic Liberal George Washington University Law Professor Jonathan Turley: *"Democrats are seeking to remove Trump on the basis of his remarks to supporters before the rioting at the Capitol. ...his address does not meet the definition for incitement under the criminal code. It would be viewed as protected speech by the Supreme Court."*

It is pelosi and Schumer who are sponsoring sedition and the goal is the downfall or destruction of America. In Turley's words, by *"now seeking an impeachment for remarks covered by the First Amendment."*

The Free Speech violation is evidenced by Twitter and other Social media platforms blacklisting the President while remaining open to posts from dictators and fascists leaders whose governments sponsor the killing of those who support or advocate for LGBTQ, female and basic human rights.

In effect, we have Pelosi and various Social Media Oligarchs engaging in fascist activities while deflecting by accusing Trump of the actions they are perpetrating – a fact you have been informed was happening throughout the four years of the Trump card series.

Turley went on to point to the hypocrisy within his own party and pointed the fact that some of his fellow *"Democrats are pushing this dangerously vague standard while objecting to their remarks given new meaning from critics."*

In effect, Turley has stated they are guilty of the very acts and accusations they throw at Trump – a standard fascist propaganda technique.

Turkey pointed out that while *"The damage caused by the rioters this week was enormous, however, it will pale in comparison to the damage from a new precedent of a snap impeachment for speech protected under the First Amendment. ... In a process of deliberative judgment, the reference to a snap impeachment is a contradiction. In this new system, guilt is not doubted and innocence is not deliberated."*

Turkey is declaring that the new system is based on the idea of being guilty as charged without any evidence or any right to a fair trial or ability to establish innocence. Rather, you are told there is "overwhelming evidence" which, of course, is never presented, and there there is the accusation of a crime without ever identifying the specific statute violated – a fact we saw in the first impeachment.

It is important to recall that the real "crime" involved was President Trump adhering to a 1998 Clinton United States Ukraine treaty to share information on corruption investigations involving citizens of the two respective nations – in that instance the Ukraine investigation into establish corrupt Burisma practices which were given international cover through the appointment of Hunter Biden and his partner to the Burisma board, with result of subsequent cover being provided by representatives of the U.S. Department of State under direction of Vice President Joe Biden – which he then boasted, on an international stage, was with the full knowledge and approval of President Barack Obama.

Should the policy of impeachment after leaving office become "the gold standard" that Pelosi and Schumer wish to set, there is a real possibility that some future Congress might decide to impeach both Biden and Obama for conspiracy resulting from bribery.

Under present conditions, as Senate leader, Schumer will rush through the first conviction in history, and individuals like Nader and Schiff will again declare "*overwhelming evidence*" that they will never need to cite or explain in a lawful manner.

However, before Schumer can convict Trump of exercising Freedom of Speech, the House will need to vote on and pass the relevant Articles of Impeachment. But Pelosi controls only 51.3% of the House vote and 66.7% is needed for passage.

As noted in need reports, Turley cited specific examples of the "*vague standard*" the Democratic leadership has now established as their means of judgment:

"*Conservatives have pointed to Maxine Waters asking her supporters to confront Republicans in restaurants, while Ayanna Pressley insisted amidst the violent marches last year that there needs to be unrest in the streets' and Kamala Harris said 'protesters should not let up' even as some of those marches turned violent.*"

The rule of law has ended, Biden is above the law, and the era of American fascism has been offered for acceptance by the masses willing to see The Emperor's New Clothes.

There is something that history will realize, even if the media does not want to admit it, one of the driving forces behind Trump's actions can be viewed in the lyrics of an old song, *"I won't Back Down"* by Tim Perry.

Well, I won't back down

No, I won't back down

You can stand me up at the gates of hell

But I won't back down

No, I'll stand my ground

Won't be turned around

And I'll keep this world from draggin' me down

Gonna stand my ground

And I won't back down

Donald John Trump does not back down – unless, by doing so, he can move forward.

In October 2015, a paperback edition of *"The Art of the Deal"* was published. A year later, Trump had defeated 16 professional politician to obtain the Republican nomination, and a month later he beat all the odds and defeated Hillary Clinton.

But we need to go back to January 2008 when he published *"Trump Never Give Up: How I Turned My Biggest Challenges into Success."* Tim Perry's song was released in September 2012 – four years after the book.

In September 2008, Trump published the paperback edition of *"Think Big: Make It Happen in Business and Life"* and again we see the guiding forces that drive the swamp and MSM crazy – we see it in a man holding the highest political office in the nation.

On 25 January, the House Managers delivered the four page Impeachment Articles to the Senate. According to Article I, Section 3 states, *"When the President of the United States is tried, the Chief Justice **shall** preside."* A former president faced a penalty reserved for a sitting President; the Swamp had the President pro tempore of the Senate, Senator Patrick Leahy, scheduled to preside while also acting as a juror. But, on 26 January it was announced the 80-year-old Leahy was hospitalized.

The Senate has no authority to hold a trial for a private citizen – the SCOTUS will, if the Senate wishes to retain an appearance of legality, need to issue a clear ruling on the Constitutionality of trying a POTUS who has already been legally removed from office.

Then there is the curious matter of the former President's legal team changing two weeks before the trial was scheduled to begin in the Senate.

Trump spokesman Jason Miller stated what was known, "*The Democrats' efforts to impeach a president who has already left office is totally unconstitutional and so bad for our country. In fact, 45 Senators have already voted that it is unconstitutional. We have done much work, but have not made a final decision on our legal team, which will be made shortly.*"

Soon after, Jonathan Turley once again wrote an opinion piece in which he voiced several opinion. One was that a Senate trial could work to the advantage of Trump. As Turley noted, it would be the first time in history that *"the House used a snap impeachment and sent the Senate no record to support its article. …Part of the controversy of this snap impeachment is using a trial solely for electoral disbarment."*

There is no question that the Constitution limits the power of the Senate and the use of impeachment. The Senate does not have the *"carte blanche authority to bar a citizen from office by majority vote."* Though, if the intend was to create a dictatorship and negate the Constitution. For the average citizen, this is not something to be condoned – it is a dangerous tactic for any who love America and the model it has served as for the global expansion of democracy.

Whatever party controls the legislature and White House – as the Democrats now control things – can bar any qualified opponents from the act of running for federal office. Challenge the realities of the election, raise doubts about mail-in ballots where voter identity is unverified, and people like Pelosi, Schumer, Waters, Schiff, and Nadler will use the tactic against any who challenge the election of Joe Biden. It is the authoritarian practice in many countries.

They could use the 14th Amendment. But that would mean they would need to actually prove their case or criminally use only a majority vote in Congress – an impeachment penalty without the burden of a conviction. But, using the 14th Amendment is too clever by half – it would establish a dangerous precedent that whoever was in power could use to bar opponents from office.

CHAPTER FIVE – Consequences

"With Postal Service on 'Verge of Collapse' and 630,000 Jobs at Risk, Trump Slammed for Refusing to Act" ~ MSM, 11 April 2020

As Biden signed his Executive Orders, MSM enjoyed various projections of massive jobs lost. Canceling the Keystone XL pipeline was to have cost tens of thousands of jobs.

But, as we know from Book 1 of this series, all the jobs were temporary. There were only 50 real jobs involved; there was also the very real risk of contaminating the largest aquifer in North America and poisoning the water supply relied upon by both a significant portion of the population and American agriculture.

As we know, it is the MSM goal to promote *The Most harm to the Most People*. It isn't MSM policy, it is the governing policy of the Swamp Denizens who are also actively attempting to undermine the American Constitution.

Intelligent voters understand that no honest Senator would move forward on Articles of Impeachment that were not presented while the cited individual was in office.

If the goal is to Block someone from holding office, then the proper means would be via legislation to be passed in the House, Senate, and ultimately signed by the sitting President. This is not a problem, the 14th Amendment provides the basis for excluding any individual from holding public office. And it only requires a simple majority vote.

This reality was stated by Bruce Ackerman, a professor of law and political science at Yale Law School, in an interview conducted during the week leading up to the inauguration: *"In the American mind, impeachment is the well-established way of condemning presidents who are assaulting the foundations of democracy."* But there is a second path created in 1868 to prevent any who promoted the Confederates cause from entering Federal politics.

The relevant portion of the 14th Amendment states:

"No person shall be a Senator or Representative in Congress, or elector of President and Vice President, or hold any office, civil or military, under the United States, or under any state, who, having previously taken an oath, ... shall have engaged in

insurrection or rebellion against the" Constitution of the United States.

Such legislation should also meet a basic test -- the targeted individual should have clearly violated the Constitution and their oath of office.

Impeachment is, by its wording, based on an issue of a morality violation involving the public trust; the specific violation must be clearly stated and defined in a way where the violation can be used as a litmus test for actions by any office holder. As the constitution states, if a crime is involved, a Senate finding of moral guilt does not introduce "Double Jeopardy" when faced with any future prosecution for any criminal element or aspect of the action that lead to impeachment.

However, if a criminal act is alleged, it should be clearly and precisely cited as part of the act of Impeachment. If it is not cited, then how could any honest Senator determine the moral infraction associated with it? And again, there need not be a statutory crime, but absent that crime, the moral standard violated must be clearly and so it can serve as a basis for judging the actions of other governmental employed, legislators, or executives.

If "incendiary" or "motivational" language is the basis for charging a moral impropriety related the crime of sedition, then anyone using such language should be held accountable. It's the morality of the classic assertion said to have motivated the killing of Thomas Beckett on 29 December 1170 – *"Will no one rid me of this meddlesome priest?"*

Curiously, given the fact that, since the announcement of the 2016 election results, Trump has been deemed to be meddlesome. Though, in his testimony before Congress, James Comey used the quote as if Trump was King Henry the Second. Comically, the King was speaking in 1170, the year when the first of the 4-Sister was born and so the year when the common link between all the Presidents was forged. Symbolically, excommunication could be seen as a form of impeachment and thus strengthen Comey's analogy.

The meddlesome nature that Trump uses to achieve things is close fit to that of the Archbishop of Canterbury, Thomas Beckett – though, Trump will not be physically assassinated, impeachment has allowed the world to witness four years of figurative attempts. The second impeachment, for the purpose of ending Trump's ability to run again in 2024, would be analogous to a political assassination.

Meanwhile, New York City continues to harass the President.

New York City Mayor Bill De Blasio, the man city official who stood shoulder-to-shoulder with BLM demonstrators defacing the street in front of Trump Tower showed his disrespect for the rule of law when, on 15 January, he announced he would be canceling City contracts with the Trump Organization.

The stated basis for his action is a "criminal act" clause in the contracts. The basis for asserting a crime having been committed and proved is the House assertion alleging that Trump committed the crime of insurrection when he told those gathered on 6 January *"So let's walk down Pennsylvania Avenue. I want to thank you all. God bless you and God bless America."*

Of course, Impeachment is not evidence of a crime, and even if there was a Senate conviction, the Constitution is clear about the need for a Court action to establish criminality.

De Blasio has acted illegally and established his disdain for the American system of justice. To be accused is not to be guilty – Americans live under a system based on the precept "innocent until proved guilty." Moreover, all corporations are legal entities unto themselves – they are no liable for the actions of their stockholders, principal owners, or family members of the firm's founders.

In the case of The Trump Organization, Wikipedia states that it *"is a group of about 500 business entities of which Donald Trump is the sole or principal owner. About 250 of these entities use the Trump name. The organization was founded in 1923 by Donald Trump's paternal grandmother, Elizabeth Christ Trump, and his father, Fred Trump, as E. Trump & Son."*

We are further informed that, in terms of any managerial responsibility, *"Donald Trump relinquished his role in the Trump Organization after the 2016 election. On January 11, 2017, he announced that he and his daughter Ivanka would fully resign and his sons Donald Jr. and Eric would take executive charge of the various businesses, along with CFO Allen Weisselberg."*

That reality reduces Donald J Trump to the role of a passive stockholder, whose activities unrelated to the firm do not conform to the nature or purpose of the termination clause. Thus, De Blasio has not only acted illegally with regard to claiming the commission of a crime, he has acted illegally in terms of the contracts with The

Trump Organization and thus opened the city to legal liability for any and all damages – be they financial loses or losses in reputation based on slandering a business entity that has existed as a mainstay of the New York City real estate industry for nearly a century.

Fox News reported, *"The mayor said that City Hall would notify the Trump Organization that it will be canceling agreements to operate the carousel in Central Park, two skating rinks and a golf course. He said the agreements for the carousel and skating rinks will be ended in less than a month, but that the golf course could take longer."*

Emphasizing his illegal rush to judgment and legal position that the accused is "guilty until proved innocent," De Blasio stated as fact, *"The president incited a rebellion against the United States government that killed five people and threatened to derail the constitutional transfer of power. The City of New York will not be associated with those unforgivable acts in any shape, way or form, and we are immediately taking steps to terminate all Trump Organization contracts."*

In response, the spokesperson for The Trump Organization said, *"The City of New York has no legal right to end our contracts and if they elect to proceed, they will owe The Trump Organization over $30 million dollars. This is nothing more than political discrimination, an attempt to infringe on the First Amendment and we plan to fight vigorously."* Thus revealing that the City could lose the $30 million in the three contracts, plus many more millions in legal fees and court costs.

As the nation moved to the Inauguration, Pelosi was planning to repeat the delay she performed with the first Impeachment and the Republican Senate Majority Leader Mitch McConnell decided to open the possibility that he would join those who disregard the Constitution and vote to convict former President Trump. However, he did inform his fellow Republican Senators that he would *"listen to the legal arguments when they are presented to the Senate."*

It was anticipated that five Senators would disregard the legal and Constitutional realities to ensure Donald John Trump received the nation's first Senate conviction, while also making him the first former-President to have a impeachment sustained by the Senate – these names would therefore be engraved in the annuls of history: Susan Collins of Maine, Lisa Murkowski of Alaska, Mitt Romney of

Utah, Ben Sasse of Nebraska, and Pat Toomey of Pennsylvania.

At least they would, if all the Democrats voted to convict and were joined in that vote by an additional eleven Republicans. The beauty of the historic second Impeachment was that it was achieved without a hearing or even a signal witness.

A week before the Inauguration, South Carolina's Republican Senator Lindsey Graham stated that, "*If President-elect Biden truly seeks unity, he has an opportunity to make a major step in that direction by rejecting post-presidential impeachment.*"

Arkansas' Republican Senator Tom Cotton remained mindful of constructionist reality: "*The Founders designed the impeachment process as a way to remove officeholders from public office – not an inquest against private citizens.*"

The delight of the situation is the devout desire of Congress to show, and prove to, the world that America is not a nation of laws at all.

Let's go back and look at aspects of both the Executive Orders and Impeachment. While going so, remember that those seeking to impeach a former President have called him a dictator. Joe Biden is on record as to what constitutes a dictator:

"Well, I got to get the votes. I got to get the votes. That's why, you know, the one thing that I — I have this strange notion, we are a democracy. Some of my Republican friends and some of my Democratic friends even occasionally say, 'Well, if you can't get the votes, by executive order you're going to do something.' Things you can't do by executive order unless you're a dictator. We're a democracy. We need consensus."

Governing by executive order is among "*Things you can't do by executive order unless you're a dictator.*" And, as the record shows, Biden has set a record for issuing Executive Orders. The real record for total orders is held by Franklin Delano Roosevelt – who was elected to four terms, served three, and was dealing with a Great depression and a World War. Over his eight years in office, Obama averaged 32 Executive Orders a year – Biden beat that number in his first three days.

Based on his own words and assessment, Biden is a dictator. And based on the nature of some of his orders, he is a Dictator who is out to harm America.

Just before 12:20 p.m., President Biden official canceled the Trump administration ban on individuals undergoing transgender transformation from serving in the military — with a stroke of the pen, Biden allowed individuals who needed daily medical care, and were therefore unfit for deployment, to be on the military payroll and receiving full government or taxpayer funding for what can only be termed elective surgery. If that is legitimate, it then follows that other military personnel should be covered for facelifts and any of the other types of available elective surgery or post surgery recovery.

Biden's order effectively weakened the military.

As we know, in his first hundred days, the hallmark of the Biden Administration is an unprecedented impeachment of a former president; this has been shown to be clearly unconstitutional by the failure of the Chief Justice to preside.

Because the impeachment will consume critical legislative time, a CNN reporter attempted to question Biden about whether impeachment would imperil his agenda, Biden did not answer. This was not a crime he was inclined to boast of.

When, as in the case of the Article I, Section 3, Constitutional wording about the impeachment of a President (be they current or former) or any legal mandate, when the word "shall" appears, it is understood by qualified lawyers and judges mean the wording that follows is an absolute mandate or governing condition.

And while other impeachments are flexible, Article I, Section 3 of the Constitution is clear that any action against a PRESIDENT shall be overseen by the Chief Justice of the Supreme Court – NOT a Senate President pro tempore acting as both judge and jurist.

Because impeachment is an act of removal from office, the Constitutional action only applies to a sitting President of one who has not already been legally removed from office.

On 3 November, Trump was legally removed from office via the election process; this was the confirmed, on 6 January, by the Electoral College count. According to law, on 20 January the Senate lost its Constitutional right to hold an impeachment trial. Though it is also arguable that the House lost the right to indict on either 3 November or 6 January – based upon whether we use a ballot based or Electoral College removal date.

Impeachment is a remedy that is intended to remove any untrustworthy or dishonest individual who has not already been legally removed from office – "legal" does not include effectively removed, as when a person resigns to avoid impeachment. This was seen in the case of Richard Nixon, where Ford pardoned him to allow him to escape both impeachment and criminal prosecution.

Should that change, every former president can be indicted, tried, convicted, and then denied all rights and privileges earned by once holding office. If not for the pardon, Richard Nixon could be tried in absentia, as could both George H.W. and George W. Bush.

Even Abraham Lincoln could be tried for his Emancipation Proclamation, which was issued when it was still constitutional to own slaves -- a legal fact which overshadows any retroactive moral assertion, even if the assertion is later Constitutionally enshrined.

The legal precedent is rather interesting. Based on the House actions, at any time, without either evidence or witnesses, the House can indict (impeach) a former POTUS based on a legal standard that would be thrown out of any honest court – but which is consistent with the actions of a fascist-dictatorship state.

Just months after the new Vice President, Kamala Harris, organized to pay the bail for rioters who violently attached and destroyed, speaking on the Senate floor for the House Managers, Representative Jamie Raskin would assert that Trump's exercise of free speech and a call to the public to voice their views had been an act where *"Donald John Trump engaged in high crimes and misdemeanors by inciting violence against the government of the United States."*

Even if it could be factually demonstrated to be true, the proper and lawful legal venue to adjudicate the charge remained the civil court and not the Senate floor. But the criminals in the House of Representatives were fully aware that no legitimate court would hear the case – which is why their Senate counterparts would move forward when the Chief Justice declined to oversee the preceding as required if the process were constitutional.

But obedience to the Constitution and due process is not something we would expect from the representative of a *"Kangaroo Court."* Any rational person would expect exactly what happened – an indictment complaint was issued, votes impeachment or indict were cast, and all without the presentation of witnesses, evidence, or opinions from qualified legal experts with regard to jurisdiction.

With its two hour *"Kangaroo Court"* impeachment, members

of the House demonstrated they no longer supports the "Rule of Law" or anything even approaching an American standard of "Due Process."

But then, Pelosi and the rest of her Swamp Denizen buddies knew full well that their actions were illegal and that they could not hold anything even arguably passing as a legal vote after the Inauguration. They knew they were violating their oath of office, so had to rush things through – their reason being that they were scared that Trump would achieve a Grover Cleveland style return and they would be denied their ability to drain the public coffers.

Under the leadership of Nancy Pelosi and Chuck Schumer, the would will come to understand that America lacks the most basic level of intelligence – it is a nation where insurrection is defined by a President tell tens of thousands of citizens *"peacefully and patriotically make your voices heard"* and to make their voices heard, *"...we're going to walk down Pennsylvania Avenue, I love Pennsylvania Avenue, and we're going to the Capitol and we're going to try and give it a try..."*

With the impeachment, Pelosi's followers have made a direct attack on American Freedom of Assembly and Freedom of Speech. There is no question that elements in the 6 January crowd we hell bent on violence – but it was the violence that Pelosi condoned when conducted by BLM and the Cancel Culture.

At its heart, Trump's rally was concerned with ensuring that American elections were properly conducted. He and his followers had heard four years of Pelosi's cabal yelling about election fraud – yet they did nothing to ensure an honest 2020 election. Rather, due to the pandemic, or using it as an excuse, they promoted mail-in ballots, early voting – so that arising issues became meaningless – and discouraged in person voting.

As a result, the election had a record number of votes and it destroyed all the existing demographic metrics for outcome results. We saw a man who could not get people to appear at rallies or watch him on TV apparently vote for him – 81.28 million of them. At the same time, the man who always had large turnouts for his events also received a record number of votes – 74.22 million.

The major difference in voting patterns was demographics – Biden's votes were heavily concentrated in those cities with excellent internet access and therefore a great deal of exposure to propaganda that had disparaged Trump for four years and finally served as basis for threats to the professional he had created over the preceding four decades.

Alan Dershowitz defined an aspect of the propaganda when he noted: "*You have to be willing to support the free speech of your enemies. ... The cancel culture is a direct frontal attack not only on freedom of speech; ... it cancels due process. It doesn't matter if you are innocent or guilty.*"

Social Media contributes to and, in many ways defined, the Cancel Culture movement that is a form of dictatorship. It thrives on blacklisting, blanket censorship, and deplatforming of any who it sees as supporting justice and historic continuity. As with the last minute, no hearings or evidence impeachment, it inflicts political retribution on those who honor treaties and the Constitution – and that introduces a threat to every patriotic America or any who seek to have rights or freedoms embodied in the American Constitution.

Twitter, the platform which profited from Trump's presence, banned the New York Post over its honest investigative journalism into the affairs of Hunter Biden. And since he would no longer be in a position of power and influence, it even banned Trump. Twitter hypocrisy was mad blatant by comparison to those it does not ban – while some of Trump's tweets might be classified as were untrue in the context of the limited characters allowed to express ideas, and they are incendiary when viewed by those whose evils he exposes, there is no question that the Ayatollah Khamenei's twitter account is far worse. Yet, Twitter supports the Ayatollah and provides him a global voice because he is not an immediate threat to the political positions of its owners.

In an interview, liberal actor Bryan Cranston defined the crux of the Cancel Culture: "*We live in this 'cancel culture' of people erring and doing wrong, either on purpose or by accident. And there is less forgiveness in our world. ... I think our societies have been harder and less understanding, less tolerant, less forgiving. ... I think we need to take a second look at that, and exhale, and realize that asking forgiveness and receiving forgiveness are not weaknesses but are human strengths.*"

Why would the forces behind the Cancel Culture destroy a statue of Columbus? As I've written in other works, he saved many Spanish Jews and helped them establish new communities in the

Americas at a time when Spanish Catholics were murdering them. The attacks on him would be like attacking Audrey Hepburn for her work with the resistence and her efforts to save Jews from death at the hands of the Nazis.

Granted, in the years after the voyages the Conquistadors and Catholic Priests followed Columbus to the New World where they killed the Mayan and chased the Jewish settlers into what is now the American Southwest. The remnants of the Spanish Counter Culture can be seen in history of modern day Mexico – a culture that became as much a failure as Spain.

We see the Counter Culture destroy historic remnants of the Old South and Confederacy. We are told it's because they rebelled against the North and supported the Constitutional Slavery which the founding fathers had negotiated into the Constitution. Curiously those same Counter Culture types exalt Lincoln's Emancipation Proclamations – an unconstitutional executive order which, in 1870, was made lawful through Constitutional Amendment. But that fact does not alter the reality of a President lacking the right or authority to simply proclaim any Article of the Constitutional void.

From both a moral and economic perspective, the South was wrong to support Slavery – slavery is simply extreme socialism; it is a master [the state] providing limited resources for the support and sustenance of workers while denying those same workers the right and freedom to engage in capitalistic activities that would benefit and advance everyone.

Imagine welfare, public assistance, or Universal Basic Income being provided with the mandate that the State would assign daily work to the recipients under the condition that they had no right to complain, resist, or engage in any activity not explicitly approved by the State on a day-to-day basis. That's slavery.

In contrast, we have Biblical Socialism – a situation where everyone has the right to choose their work or the way they spend their time, as dictated by environment constraints, where the State ensures the individuals have those individuals have the food, shelter, medical support, and education necessary for them to achieve their goals.

To a limited degree, the "stimulus package" associated with the Coronavirus pandemic (or past recessions and depressions) can be seen as limited Biblical Socialism. Of course, those who serve

Satan will wave the Bible and oppose its socialistic mandates. They ignore the fact that, in the New Testiment, Jesus was so confident in the people obeying socialism that he could tell his followers to dispose of their assets and rely upon the kindness of those to whom they brought the message.

Those who do not recall the direction might want to reference Matthew 19:21 where Jesus says: "*If you want to be perfect, go, sell your possessions and give to the poor, and you will have treasure in heaven. Then come, follow Me. ... If you want to be perfect, go, sell your possessions and give to the poor, and you will have treasure in heaven. Then come, follow me.*"

Two thousand years ago, the responsibility of caring for your neighbor – reciprocal assistance – was an individual responsibility; the leaders of the State were only concerned with warfare, conquest, and the acquisition of personal power or wealth. In modern society, the governmental leaders are supposed to represent us and deliver the neighborly assistance in the most efficient manner possible.

One of the consequences of the 2020 election was a decision by Andrew Yang – who failed in his attempt to be a candidate – to oppose Bill De Blasio's incompetent leadership and run for Mayor of New York City. Yang's economic platform includes a variation on Universal Basic Income scaled back to create a municipal-scale plan that promises to revitalize New York at a time when it is among the top three locations in America that is losing population – it is being abandoned because of the systemic hatred for those, like Trump, who have made it an economic powerhouse.

Yang's concept would add UBI to the city's Human Resources Administration programs and grant roughly 500,000 New Yorkers in the greatest need an annual $2,000 - $5,000 in disposable cash income.

Given the normal economic multiplier range of 7-10, these funds would increase the city's annual Gross Domestic Product by 17.5-25 Billion dollars. In theory, the compounded increase in tax revenue from the businesses where the money is spent would cover the full cost and return a profit to the city. Because the poor are generally situated in locations that depend of small mom-and-pop stores, the UBI would go to ensure the survival of those stores. And because it would not have the restrictions commonly associated with assistance programs, it would allow families with children to obtain items that could help those children advance.

The objective is to address systemic poverty. Delivery of the UBI funds would be through a "People's Bank" bank account that would be connected to the city's IDNYC – a municipal identification card for New York City residents, ages 10 and up, which assists in the obtaining access to New York City services that require some form of recognized identification. The ulitmate result would be a functional "Trickle Up" economy.

However, New York's Jewish community might understand that Yang will be opposed by those who would say *"Mozhish, da nye khotchish."* It is the appropriate response to the Conservative far-right who find excuses not to help shore-up the foundation of the economy – *"You can, you just don't want to!"*

For those who have difficulty understanding, consider what has been the global economic response to the pandemic and need for restrictions that detrimentally affect earnings.

Everywhere we look, except in the supposedly richest nation in history, governments have reasoned with stimulus packages that ensured a continuation of monthly income.

As has previously been cited in this series, there is economic evidence that a UBI would save the government money. At the base level, it would eliminate the need for Public Assistance welfare. It would also allow an elimination of the "Personal Deduction" on tax forms – increasing the earned income subject to taxes and related tax revenues.

As mentioned, the standard economic multiplier would then see seven to ten time the amount added to the GDP or deposited in savings which then become available for conventional loans. If it is invested, it grows industry and wealth – and, upon liquidation of the profitable investments, it generates Capital Gains Tax revenues.

The costly problem comes when a bureaucracy is created to restrict who will get the money – when funds not truly "universal." New York City could have that problem, unless the distribution is handled through the tax authority and paid only to those who file an annual return.

Yang's "People's Bank" account system will serve the same purpose as a tax filing. It will, as we saw with the stimulus, provide a means of direct deposit and immediate access which allows things to be automated – and provides a necessary record of who received the funds. The "People's Bank" then provides a debt card attached to a social security number and the ability of illegals or non-existent individuals to scam funds is diminished.

It can be done. But as the phrase states, *"You can, you just don't want to!"* You do not want to have a "Star Trek" economy and a culture where there is no poverty. Poverty ensures there is always "the other" who can be disparaged and blamed for problems; it also provides a defacto slave and criminal class.

A few decades before the United States was founded, Rabbi Israel ben Eliezer – known as the Baal Shem Tov and founder of the Hasidic Jewish tradition – stated, *"When we do not want to do the right thing, our evil inclination convinces us that we are unable to do so. If only we would wish to do what we know we should, we would find ourselves capable."*

Over 260 years have passed since the Baal Shem Tov's death and little has changed. The refusal to do the right thing can take on many forms – Right-wing Conservatives who yell *"Right to Life"* are happy to promote military actions in foreign lands, where foreign lives are taken; when a condom breaks, they insist upon the women having the child, but then they disparage her if she cannot afford proper prenatal or perinatal care, or if she cannot afford to support the child.

On 29 January, JAMA published a study on *"Insurance and Perinatal Health Care Use Among Low-Income US Women"* during the period 5-7 years after passage of the 2010 Affordable Care Act {ACA} and established its failure to reach those who lacked proper care at a critical point in the development of their successor generation's development – from gestation through first year of life.

Without saying so, the study revealed the gross hypocrisy and therefore the devout Satanic service of those who proclaim to be pro-life, but who also oppose government provided healthcare for the lives they insist be born. On another pro-Satan level, apart from those supporting Universal Healthcare, these people comprise a bipartisan faction that routinely displays contempt for an underlying biblical concept embodied in "the Good Samaritan" – irregardless of their true economic state, those who are in need, even if it is only temporary, must receive assistance.

In the case of the population studied by the paper, we are told by the authors:

"The study sample consisted of 39 378 women with a mean (SD) age of 27.4 (5.9) years. Of these, 43.6% were continuously insured, 21.3% experienced shifts between private coverage and Medicaid, 32.8% experienced shifts between insurance and uninsurance, and 2.4% were continuously uninsured."

We are also told that 60.1% of the continuously uninsured category were Spanish-speaking Hispanic women. Given that the nation's largest minority group (16.7%) are Hispanic, it follows that the racist denial of care would be more highly represented among that group.

The study determined that the very act of *"Improving receipt of recommended maternity care among women who experience uninsurance in the perinatal period is a clinical and policy priority. Adoption of the Patient Protection and Affordable Care Act's Medicaid expansion has improved perinatal insurance continuity for low-income women."*

For those who support a Biden-Pelosi-Schumer open border policy, the Satanic effect is to enhance the segment denied care, and thus to create a generation of children who a medical inferior to the current majority. In talking of the 16.7%, we are discussing roughly 52 million people of which 47 million are citizens. Demographically, they are younger than the general population. And because of the way school funding is managed, they are also less educated, which means they are also less wealthy – and more likely to remain so. As a result the ultimate effect is to drag down economic growth and so create an opportunity for China to replace America on the global stage – both economically and politically.

As you were told in 2017, Donald John Trump was trying to prevent the Chinese expansion and takeover. Now that the White House is occupied by a Manchurian Candidates who is supported by the anti-Trump faction in Congress, we can judge America's future simply by examining beginning-of-life healthcare and how it might be reinforced through education. Not only primary education, but the cost and availability of higher education.

If a child's development is impeded through a lack of health care in their initial formative stage, can we really believe they will go on to be a Rafael Edward Cruz or Amanda S. C. Gorman and attend Harvard – with or without a crushing student loan debt? Or are they more likely to be incarcerated before the age of twenty-five?

A second 29 January article, *"Racial Inequities in Pediatric Emergency Care,"* informs us the current findings *"are consistent with decades of previous research documenting inequalities in health care delivery based on race/ethnicity."* As we have heard from AOC during rate moments of lucid adult presentation, these inequities "must be examined in the context of inequities within the social framework of a community," and *"The driving force behind disparities in health care delivery is multifactorial."* And the results of the systemic inequities propagated in areas like AOC's NYC district have contributed to both the high Covid-19 case rate and accompanying high fatality rate among AOC's constituents.

Biden was there for the adoption of ACA, and for the placing of children in cages at the border – as shown in photographs from 2014 which MSM attributed to Trump, who took office three years later. Now, President Biden is exercising his Executive Powers in a way that, at first glance, seems designed to harm the nation and do nothing for those who need critical medical at the various stages in the normal life-cycle – starting with conception and extending into pandemics which will only become more common as climate change continues.

If we view Presidential Executive Orders as routine executive responsibility, we can equate them to rights and responsibilities in the private sector, with Congress serving the role of the Corporate Board of Directors.

Within that construct, ACA benefits, which must be paid for through premiums becomes an accounting issue. The premiums are simply an "accounts receivable" item; if handled as they would be in standard private sector accounting practice, The POTUS or CEO, as managing executive, could allow their accrual. He could then direct the "bookkeeper" to send an invoice concurrent with the issuance of annual "tax documents" so that the accrued premiums could then be paid from, or charged against, after tax income when the debtor files their annual taxes.

Curiously, if the premiums are a deductible medical expense – defined along with other medical expenses under current law – it follows that there the cost would be deducted and there would be "a wash," meaning nothing is payable and, if the amount do does not exceed any refund, the government keeps any "refund" as satisfying the debt.

If the taxpayer contributed the monthly amount, they would not have an "accounts payable" and would simply deduct what was paid – in effect being reimbursed based on their tax bracket. During disruptions in income of the type associated with the corona virus pandemic, a major recession, or a depression, this system would be highly beneficial to the economy and health of the nation.

Congress could object, or they could approve with a simple vote which would have those opposed to a healthy population and nation could go on record. However, since debt collection or record keeping is not a defined role of the Congress, but actually falls under the Executive Branch, the only issue related to an Executive Order establishing "accounts receivable" process would whether it could be deemed a element of the Income Tax process. The Chief executive could decide to allow it to accrue and, when the individual dies, have the DOJ file a claim against the debtors estate.

Right-wing Conservatives and Left-wing Satanic hypocrites both love to watch people die, often they even promote the murder of foreign nationals. Many are angry at Trump because he was the first President in recent history who has not engaged in a new war or expand an existing one. That deep desire to kill foreigners knows no party line – both Clinton and Obama were responsible for many deaths.

As the media has shown, Nancy Pelosi and her ilk considered the riots, burning, and killing in Seattle and other locations to be simple "Democracy" at work. And, as we saw on 6 January, they are fully in favor of violence – so long as it does not knock on their door or is confined to a neighboring state.

Historically, since World War Two, when FDR was forced by the attack on Pearl Harbor to join the war, only Lyndon B. Johnson, Richard M. Nixon, and Gerald R. Ford did not start any wars. But, to be fair, Johnson and Nixon had Vietnam to play with, and Ford was the first unelected president in the nation's history.

That he was unelected imposed some constants on his ability to initiate a war, as did the fact that he had to ease the nation out of the tensions associated with the anti-Vietnam War movement and the mess associated with both Watergate and his decision to pardon Nixon. Effectively, that mess was all the war he could handle.

Trump had his war – it was domestic and initiated by Swamp Denizens who were angry at not having Hillary serving them. What we have seen for five years is an adversarial universe that is swiftly heading for implosion. It isn't just in the United States. At the same time the Swamp began its attacks of Trump, the United Kingdom was voting to exit the European Union and abandon an economic pact that was supporting it and allowing it to function smoothly.

It has been is said, *"where man eats man and only the most brutish survive."* The political system of both England and America have degraded into a "dog eat dog" or "man devour man" existence and threatens to end the only remaining two nations governed by descendants of Charlemagne through the 4-Sisters.

For America, we add the fact they are, with a couple of minor exceptions, also POTUS Cousins. But even the exceptions tend to be married to POTUS Cousins.

CHAPTER SIX – New Game

"'He is well aware this is the most important inaugural speech since Lincoln,' said Sen. Chris Coons"

As Trump prepared to leave office, he signed an order lifting coronavirus-related international travel restrictions for Brazil, most of Europe, Ireland, and United Kingdom. It would then fall upon Biden to reinstate those orders and add the CDC requirement for all air travelers to show negative COVID-19 testing before entering the US.

In the meantime, on Inauguration day, a HUFFPOST article – that was entitled "Trump reportedly considers exacting revenge on Republicans by forming his own party" – included a video, "Trump Packs Up His Desk", including a segment stating, *"predictably, late night hosts cracked jokes about the departure"* and then cut to Jimmy Kimmel stating he *"would sign up for a streaming service that showed nothing but Trump's stuff being moved out of the White House."*

The segment then cut to Seth Meyers saying, *"I sure hope someone is watching him pack because he's definitely going to try to steal stuff. Sir, why is the bust of Lincoln being packed away?"* Meyers then did a lamb impression of Trump saying *"Uh, what? No, this is mine from home."*

Meyers' line was immediately followed by the report stating, *"Coincidently, footage later surfaced of Lincoln's bust leaving the White House, raising eyebrows."* Then, immediately cutting back to Kimmel viewers were shown "an unidentified trio" carrying the bust of Lincoln past a Marine Sargent who was hold the door for them – his uniform was decorated with four medals.

And Kimmel stated *"Is it possible that Trump is looting the White House before he goes? He's going to use that as a hood ornament on his golf cart."*

Having the time to emphasize how "comics" slandered the outgoing President, viewers were then told that, on 14 January, The White House Historical Association *"certified some items removed had been on loan from other collections."*

Slander and defamation of charter have been the hallmark of the entertainment and MSM for the previous five years. When dealing with unfounded speculation for the purpose of defaming an individual and, in so doing, seeking to undermine the credibility of the American government, the "comic" media has the advantage of being able to assert, "I was just joking."

But the subliminal long-term damage they do is not a joke.

The article stated Trump was floating the idea of creating a new political party that would be called "The Patriot Party."

Life goes on and, via Instagram, Tiffany Trump announced her engagement to Michael Boulos – who was born in Lebanon, his family business is in Nigeria and he's about four years her junior. It is interesting that, with this marriage, Tiffany will probably be the richest member of the Trump clan.

The events leading up to and on 19 January 2021 marked an end to the first phase of the historic transition. Then, with Biden's inauguration the nation moved into a new phase in which the rule of law would crumble.

On 26 January, Rand Paul stood on the Floor of the Senate and denounced the hypocrisy exhibited by the dying breed of Left-wing Swamp Denizens.

Paul pointed out there were *"700 law enforcement officers injured during Antifa riots"* and that the riots included *"at least 19 murders, including retired police officer David Dorn."*

Paul then challenged Democrats on whether *"they had ever given a speech that says 'take back, fight for your country.' Who hasn't used the word 'fight' figuratively?"* He then want to know if we *"are going to put every politician in jail, are we going to impeach every politician who uses the words 'fight' figuratively?*

Granted, it would be nice to impeach and jail any politician who engaged in a figurative call to violent action which was then followed by violent action – any politician caught in the "*Will no one rid me of this meddlesome priest?*" trap.

But in the case of Trump, we know the destructive violence was planned long before he gave his speech, and that it had nothing to do with him or his speech. We also know the Capital Police were aware of the planned violence and that Pelosi claims she was never informed of the security danger – meaning the Police failed in their duty, or Pelosi is once again a liar endangering the lives or her fellow Representatives for personal benefit. Pelosi needed the violence to use as a political tool. With it, she could be ensured months of distraction from the actions of Biden during his first hundred days.

As tweeted by Representative Marjorie Taylor Greene:

"Jan 24: When thousands of angry protesters stormed the Capitol in Madison, WI 10 yes ago, @SpeakerPelosi supported the violent attack.

'Protesters ripped the hinges of an antique oak door at the State Street entrance and streamed inside...a sea of thousands had flooded the capitol.'

'Police found dozens of .22-caliber bullets scattered across the Capitol grounds. The occupiers drew chalk outlines of fake dead bodies etched with Walker's name on the floor, and carried signs that read "Death to tyrants," "The only good Republican is a dead Republican"'

"With all the violence and death threats to Gov Walker, his family, and Republican Senators @SpeakerPelosi doubled down on her support of the violent #insurrection at the Wisconsin Capitol.

"...the leader of the #HouseOfHypocrites led the impeachment of President Trump.

"'Flashback: ... Pelosi praised unionists storming Wisconsin State Capitol House Speaker Nancy Pelosi has gone on record praising the storming of the Capitol as an "impressive show of democracy in action" -- the 2011 invasion of the Madison, Wis., state capitol, that is. foxnews.com"'

Through her own actions, House Speaker Nancy Pelosi has encouraged or incited – certainly condoned – massive violence. And she has also encouraged superspreader events that would eventually lead to the massive outbreak of Covid-19 in Southern California.

Of course, we can ask if Representative Greene has performed any better. Certainly there are those who think not and have called for her removal. But that does not change the inherent reality of a House leadership bent on destroying *"the Rule of Law"* adherence to the Constitution, while engaging in legislative games intended to undermine the economy and the very foundation of America.

Remember, Pelosi believes Trump should be impeached for extolling the idea that citizens should, as they did during the 1960s, March on Washington and let their voices be heard. At the same time, she openly praised *"the storming of the [Wisconsin] Capitol as an 'impressive show of democracy in action'"* – a position that she held a during the Obama era when she was opposing the 2006 Secure Fence Act – what Trump referred to as the border security wall – being constructed by Obama.

Interestingly, since 1988, Wisconsin voted Democratic, with the only exception being its preference for Donald over Hillary in 2016. As we know, it was an exception that could be easily explained by the adherence to the POTUS Cousin/4-Sisters pattern that has controlled all American elections since the founding of the nation.

On 14 January 2021, the Washington Post ran an piece by Columnist Marc A. Thiessen entitled, *"Opinion: Democrats were for occupying capitols before they were against it."* In that article, without specifically drawing the analogy, Thiessen describes the events in Madison, Wisconsin as identical to those witnessed on 6 January 2021 in Washington, D.C.. The playbook was the one Pelosi had praised. And with that praise, the January insurrection was the one Pelosi had nurtured and expressed approval for.

As cited in book 3 of this series, in 2006, Pelosi said, *"'Drain the swamp' means to turn this Congress into the most honest and open Congress in history. That's my pledge — that is what I intend to do."* The idea of draining the swamp dates back at least to 1903, when Winfield Romeo Gaylord wrote, *"Socialists are not satisfied with killing a few of the mosquitoes which come from the capitalist swamp. They want to drain the swamp."*

So we have a socialist goal being supported by Nancy Pelosi and then adopted by Donald Trump – and Pelosi then objects to his doing what she promised would be done a decade before Trump was inaugurated. The playbook is all confused. Pelosi is the swamp and represents Swamp Denizens. The "New Game" is the same old game with the players lying to the voters.

The Republicans have pejorative, RINO, Republican In Name Only. It might well be past the time when we Democrats should be speaking of DINOs – Democrats In Name Only – who provide us the benefit of also calling the Dinosaurs, because they seem to be locked into a Silent Generation mindset that predates the Progressive ideas which were introduced by FDR. That FDR took the ideas from the Republicans becomes a historic comic reality.

As we know, on 22 June 2017, Pelosi explained her technique

for deceiving the public: *"'You smear somebody with falsehoods and all the rest, and then you merchandise it. And then [the reporters] write it, and then they say, 'See, it's reported in the press that this, this, this, and this.' So they have that validation that the press reported the smear, and then it's called the 'wrap-up smear.' And now I'm going to merchandise the press's report on the smear that we made. 'It's a tactic. And it's self-evident.'"*

The technique is classic propaganda. In modern parlance, it is a way to make something go viral. To promote a lie, you need to have an accepted information source to quote. Sometimes you are lucky and the MSM bites when the line is first cast; other times, you need to stand in the water and repeatedly cast the line. If the fish are there, and hungry, there will always be one dumb enough to bite the fly. The "New Game" is the same old game with the players lying to the voters.

Some of the rules of the "Old Game" are self-evident – those in power will be opposed by those who have lost their power.

Neither side is going to cooperate with the other. There shall be no bipartisan effort to help the voters who have been hurt by the pandemic lockdowns. And there certainly will be bipartisan attempt to correct the loss of purchasing power associated with the minimum wage – which, if it were to have the buying power it had when the last Baby-Boomer was born (in 1965), would be $20 an hour.

But let's face reality, Congress doesn't care. Pelosi seems to be using her position to garner information that can be transferred into highly profitable stock trades – in another world, the use of any knowledge known only to Congressional Committees, would qualify as a form insider trading. But not in Pelosi's world – a world that is above and immune from the law or rational conduct.

Congress should be helping citizens survive the disruption of everyday life caused by a culling virus where 40% of the victims are from the 1% of the population residing in nursing homes where they were waiting to die.

On 17 April 2020, Trump called-out 'Do Nothing Democrats' – typified by *Crazy Nancy Pelosi, Cryin' Chuck Schumer* – for their failure to *"immediately come back to Washington and approve legislation to help families in America."* To escape responsibilities, they were on an *"ENDLESS VACATION!"* And Trump was telling MSM, "We can begin the next front in our war, which we are calling

'Opening Up America Again. To preserve the health of Americans, we must preserve the health of our economy."

Ten months later, in February 2021, they repeated their love for vacations, and then returned to avoid their responsibilities with their focus on an unconstitutional impeachment. Change the name, it remains the same. So long as they get their paycheck, Congress has no interest in keeping the economy alive and healthy.

If we look at European nations, we see weekly checks being sent to ensure a stable economic foundation persists. In the riches nation in the world, it is apparently too expensive to create a solid economic foundation. But, that same nation can afford to support other nations with monetary gifts, grants, or "assistance" – paid for with tax money from the same citizens it cannot afford to support.

A study published on 13 April 2020 in the Proceedings of the National Academy of Sciences, placed the cost of the health impacts caused by air pollution at over $886 billion a year. Over 100,000 Americans die each year from air pollution caused heart attacks, strokes and other illnesses. That means that every year the nation blows half the money in the Biden $1.9 Trillion Stimulus package – at a time when Covid-19 is being credited for 469,000 deaths, most of which would have happened anyway.

One of the beauties of the pandemic is that the air has become significantly cleaner. So the dead from pollution are now attributed to Covid-19 triggering the existing damage. It is a very New Game.

Globally, Air pollution kills almost 8.8 million people a year. For the year ending in February 2021, Covid-19 is credited with less than 2.4 million. Not having Green Energy is therefore killing about four times as many people as the pandemic. And the beauty is, we don't really care – we certainly aren't showing the appropriate level of concern. At least not if we use the response to the Culling Virus as a baseline for judging the response to Air Pollution.

In April 2020, Hawaii's Democratic Senator Brian Schatz went on record criticizing the Trump administration's handling of the Covid-19 testing: "*Pandemic response has to be coordinated and paid for at the federal level. States don't have the labs, the control over the supply chain for testing and other equipment, the scientific and health research agencies, or the money to handle this without strong federal leadership.*"

With Biden in the Oval Office, have the states suddenly found the resources to handle vaccinations? Is that why so many doses are going bad or being wasted – is it that the states lack the resources?

When Biden was hiding in his basement, he set the standard by which Trump, and now he, must now be judged. H claimed that *"The president says he takes no responsibility. He's president of the United States of America. Coordinating this effort is the president's responsibility. That approach that he's taking now isn't working."*

As President, with several vaccines to chose from, under Biden's leadership, significant numbers of doses are being wasted – they are spoiling before they can be utilized. And the waste is specifically because the President has not assumed full responsibility for determining who will receive the doses. Instead, he is doing what Trump complained about – that the responsibility for distribution and inoculation has been vested in states and local municipalities.

In Willy Wonka mode, as covered in the first books of this series, Trump asserted his authority over the States. As with the obstinate girl in the story, the states pushed back and demanded to do what they wanted. As a result, consistent with Wonka, Trump simply passed the buck to them.

Metrics-driven guidelines allowed governors to make their own decisions, and the next day Trump showed his kinship with the "Oompa-Loompas" of the "LIBERATE" movement who demanded the opening of local and state economies in defiance their states' governors to restrict movement and large gatherings. Eventually, it was recognized that masks and social distancing served a purpose, but states still closed facilities that could have remained open.

Having said Trump lacked "total authority" to decide how the states return to a semblance of normalcy, he then placed obstinate governors, like New York's Andrew Cuomo, in the position of crying *"We cannot do this without the federal government."*

But, when the federal government became involved, those same governors again ignored reality – a fact we see with the rules that have almost made it impossible to utilize vaccines. Where is Joe Biden? What will he do – probably when it is too late – to correct the problem?

In reality, it was recognized that testing must be done to determine the extent of spread. Logically, this would be something that should be federally coordinated and controlled. Distributing the vaccine and inoculating the population should be federally done using state personnel and resources.

Biden complained that Trump*"takes no responsibility"* for things he was denied the authority to control. Since they want the authority, states must assume the responsibility and related costs. If their economies collapse, it's on them. But the federal government must ensure the welfare of the average citizen. Most of the states have shown they don't care about the average citizen – they do care about the non-citizen bodies that can be counted, but have no vote, and therefore can gerrymander representative power to divert or funnel federal money into elite state coffers.

Poor Biden, *"He's president of the United States of America. Coordinating this effort is the president's responsibility."* And as we watch the President sign his Executive Orders, it is becoming clear that the *"approach that he's taking now isn't working."*

It's a New Game and the rules are the ones Biden set down for Trump.

In the background, we have something that was pointed out, on 12 January, by Conservative commentator Candace Owens: *"If you legitimately won 80 million votes and were really the most popular American president of all time – why would you need to censor the voices of your political opponents & half your country?"*

Both Trump and Biden set records. The problem being that it appears that Biden voters were not voting for Biden, they were following the propaganda – seeing the *Emperor's New Clothes* – and voting against Trump.

CHAPTER SEVEN – Challenge

"A $1 billion increase in SNAP spending results in a boost to gross domestic product of $1.5 billion and helps support more than 13,000 jobs." ~ 2021 USDA study

For Biden to be a successful president, he must exceed the achievements of the man Bernie Sanders has classified as "the worst President in history."

What things need Biden exceed, what records must be set by his Administration? The obvious answer lays with the things people point to as Trump "achievements":

- 7 million new jobs
- Lowest unemployment in U.S. history
- Record low female & Minority unemployment
- Record high female & Minority employment
- No New Wars & troops from old ones withdrawn
- ISIS destroyed
- Terrorist Leaders Killed
- U.S. Embassy in Jerusalem – Israel's Capitol
- Middle East Peace & Treaties with Israel
- 230 judges confirmed & 3 SCOTUS Judges
- Exited bogus Paris Climate Accords
- Texas Solar generates more energy than coal
- Solar growing across the nation
- Energy Independence
- Gas prices cut in half
- Stock Markets make record highs & after pandemic caused crash, markets exceeded previous highs
- Record low poverty
- Record high home ownership
- Blue Collar wages increased by 16%
- Increased Border Security
- 480 miles of fence added to 2006 Secure Fence Act mandate & existing fencing upgraded to steel slats

    As of the inauguration, about ten million American citizens

were unemployed, millions were dealing with food shortage issues, numerous Americans were, by government order, deprived of their ability to work and earn money for rent and mortgages, and there were countless others facing medical related issues unrelated to the pandemic.

One of Biden's first acts was to cancel Trump's order lowering the cost of both insulin and epinephrine (adrenaline); another was an effective halt to the legislation needed for the promised $2,000 additional stimulus which he had first reduced to $1,400.

And while there is a claim that his cancellation of stopping of the Keystone XL permits could cost 52,100 jobs, as readers of this book series know, the permit was a bad idea and endangered a major portion of the regions responsible for American agricultural production and the economic power it contributes to international Balance of Payments.

As mentioned in book one of this series, *NO TRUMP CARD* {April 2017}, *"Republicans cheered the repeal of the Clean Streams legislation and the endangering of major aquifers by the Executive Order approving the Keystone XL and Dakota crude oil pipelines."*

Early on, the series also told you, *"With Donald authorizing the Keystone XL pipeline, which endangers the largest clean water aquifer in the nation, it was up to Republicans in Congress to basically authorize pollution of 6,000 miles of streams and 52,000 acres of forests in their effort to pollute drinking water..."*

We should acknowledge that the only reason Trump issued the pipeline permits was to have Canada agree to the USMCA treaty. Comically, Trump knew the Executive Order could be revoked, thus it meant nothing once the $8 Billion investment had been made and paid. [Swamp Denizens forget the Trump tactic they usually assert when they are seeking to make derogatory attacks on Trump.]

We have some of the Trump accomplishments, and some of his Keystone XL type disasters. So let's see what harms Biden added with the nearly thirty-three Executive Orders he issued in his first 75 hours in office:

- Appears to be ending American Energy Independence
- Gave Canada grounds for a lawsuit over Keystone XL by canceling pipeline permit – which Washington Post of 6 August 2012 described as low grade oil to Texas to be refined. Oil grade is so por that it doesn't justify a refinery in Canada;

the pipeline path threatens the largest aquifer in the USA – and with it most Midwest agriculture. This was a good Executive Order.

- Gave Texas grounds for a lawsuit

- Did nothing to address the leftists who are burning and rioting in Portland and Seattle, Washington.

- Moved National Guard from their accommodation in the Capitol and made them sleep on a concrete garage floor with only one available toilet.

- Damaged school sports with a order that transgender boys are to be allowed to compete on girls teams and against girls – genetically, the boys have an advantage which is equivalent to chemical induced ones that are outlawed.

- Biden overturned Trump's ban on transgender people serving in the U.S. military. That's fine if the surgery was before enlistment, but it impacts the military if it occurs while serving.

- Federal property mask mandate whose benefit may or may not be proven, but only seems to formalize what is already in place.

- Ordered illegals to be counted for the purpose of the census allocation of Representatives. As previously covered in this series, this is stupid and equates to the counting of foreign tourists.

- Biden reversed an alleged racist Trump "Muslim Ban" and then imposed a similar ban on non-US citizens traveling from South Africa. Where Trump referenced ongoing terrorist activities, Biden used the COVID-19 variant as his justification. However, the variant is in the UK, which caused Biden to reinstate the travel ban for the United Kingdom, Brazil, Ireland, and much of Europe.

- Halted student loan forgiveness programs – breaking a campaign promise.

- As mentioned, he broke the $2,000 stimulus promise and in doing so showed he also lacked leadership.

- However, Biden sought to send money to Central American nations to provide services that are needed in American and being denied to its citizens.

- Biden took a page out of the Republican playbook and issued an EO that would close various loopholes in existing "Buy American" provisions of federal contract guidelines – waivers would gain transparency.

- In March 2020, Biden unveiled a plan to "safely reopen" the nation, within the first week of his administration he seemed to be moving in that direction. Back in March he claimed: "*As we prepare to reopen America, we have to remember what this crisis has taught us: The administration's failure to plan, to prepare, to honestly assess and communicate the threat to the nation led to catastrophic results. We cannot repeat those mistakes. Make no mistake: An effective plan to beat the virus is the ultimate answer to how we get our economy back on track. So we should stop thinking of the health and economic responses as separate. They are not.*"

- There is the issue of the Stimulus which is accompanied by moves for UBI; Biden is a consistent Catholic and, in April 2020, the Pope's Easter Letter advocated for Universal Basic Income: "*This may be the time to consider a universal basic wage which would acknowledge and dignify the noble, essential tasks you carry out. It would ensure and ...achieve the ideal, at once so human and so Christian, of no worker without rights.*"

- Biden proposed an increase in Food-Stamp Benefits of 15% to address food insecurity hardship created by the pandemic.

As we move forward, it appears Biden lied when he made the various campaign promises. But he also has a history of setting a standard that he now must keep – at least, if he plans to leave or in some way approach a legacy worthy of a President.

In contrast, Trump was branded as incompetent and a liar whose political semantics were attacked by the same media that welcomed those lies when told by Pelosi, Nadler, Schiff, Schumer, and Sander's Progressives. Trump seems to have kept his campaign promises and goals – the most important one being to place America First. Curiously, Biden withing days of taking office, Biden adopted the same America First policy.

A few of Trump's promises are:

- Protecting Religious Freedom

- Raising tariffs on imported goods to protect American

producers of similar products or make it economic to return outsourced production to domestic locations.

- Related promise was to end outsourcing and retain domestic production. Internally, we see States like California and New York will be losing industries to Texas and Florida because they follow Biden policies.

- The Southern Border Wall, which is the Obama 2006 Secure Fence Act – fighting California opposition we saw Trump complete 480 new miles, and now Biden has abandoned the Obama/Democratic project that we saw Candidate Ronald Reagan oppose in 1980. So we can record Trump completing a Democratic goal, while Biden is adhering to a Reagan-Republican open border policy.

- Trump reformed the Department of Veterans Affairs and established respect for those who serve in the military – Biden would have them sleep on concrete floors in unheated locations while they are protecting him in Washington, D.C.

- Trump was bringing Troops home from combat zones related to undeclared wars; Biden seems to be ready to send them back.

- Trump ended Obamacare's individual mandate - a tax on those who could not afford health insurance.

- Trump ended the Trans-Pacific Trade Partnership and instituted United States-Mexico-Canada Agreement {USMCA} – described as a mutually beneficial win for North American workers, farmers, ranchers, and businesses. Part of the agreement established a $16 per hour wage for all firms trading across borders. It therefore has a minimum wage that is a dollar higher than the one paid in Washington, D.C. and suggested by Biden.

- EPA Reform

- Expanded America's energy sector and made America energy independent.

- Canceled the Paris Climate Agreement which is being violated by the remaining signatories. Biden has said he will rejoin it and thus partake in the political optics hoax.

- Under Trump, renewable energy production grew at a record pace – and it did so, even while Trump was ignoring "Climate

Change" as a motivator. Trump's apparent logic was that renewable energy and electric vehicles make solid economic sense, so the goal is to allow them to grow at their own pace and not place any international constraints on development.

- Electric Vehicles {EV} are on track to be prevalent in time for the 2025 Inauguration. General Motors {GM} will produce a significant number of EV by 2023, and Tesla is, of course, already producing EV.

China has a target of 2025 for its EV, and that corresponds to GM's projections. GM's target goes a step further and projects that even the production of its EV will be carbon neutral by 2040 – the Paris Climate Accord is functioning with a goal of 2050; that means Trump's America had a higher standard than the agreement that Biden wants to rejoin.

When Trump left office, his approval rating was lower than that of Reagan, GHW Bush, GW Bush, Clinton, and Obama. But, he was also the only one in that group who did not initiate of expand a war. It took GW Bush two terms to achieve an approval rating lower than Trump's.

Wartime Presidents tend to have solid approval ratings – as we know, Americans love to kill foreigners; they love to spend money on military weapons designed for indiscriminate mass slaughter. It is an American trait that they approve of killing but not of education or medical care for their citizens.

Biden enters office charged with fighting a war against Covid-19, and his approval rating is comparable to the high achieved by GW Bush when he lied to justify murdering Saddam Hussein. Biden immediately was confronted by several new strains of Covid, and no way of properly addressing them without destroying the economy.

Every other advanced nation cares for its elderly, and readily provides real support for its citizens. Americans denounce that as "Socialism" and then complain when the poor they created through their selfishness need assistance. We hear in opposition to abortion – labeled "pro-life" – for the same hypocrites who yell that women should not have children they cannot afford. And then they go a step further and deny the prenatal and postnatal care necessary to ensure the children they demand must be born are born healthy to healthy mothers.

The Most Harm to the Most People – it does seem to be the

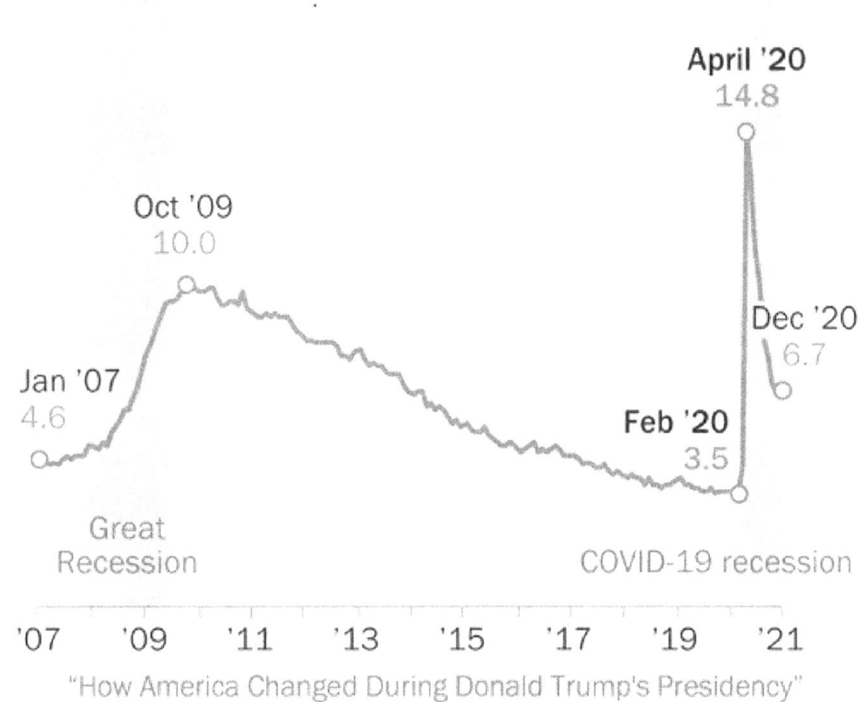

American way of life. Worse, it is done in the least cost effective way and thereby ensures greater harm.

Since we do not support children, our society has decided not to have any and we are deeply committed to the type of Baby-Bust that ensures a population decline. But we compensate by screaming for open borders and the introduction to prolific reproducers who lack the educations and skills need to support themselves and make valuable contributions to the economic survival of the nation.

If we look at unemployment – seen on PEW Research chart – we see the Bush recession forced Obama-Biden to deal with a 10% unemployment rate. We also see it took a decade for that rate to reach the 3.5% achieved at the end of Trump's third year. Then we have the pandemic caused spike to 14.8% and the eight months it took to return the rate to 6.7% – a level it took Obama-Biden over four years to obtain from a rate that was 4.8 points lower than where Trump started.

If Biden can maintain Trump's progress, the rate should be back to 3.5% by the end of summer 2021. However, there are clear indications that Biden's Executive Orders were designed to stop the Trump progress.

On 25 January, Biden affirmed his belief there was a need for the Senate to hold the Impeachment Trial.

He told CNN, it *"has to happen"* and would be *"a worse effect if it didn't happen."* And while he wouldn't publically admit it, there can be little doubt he knows the is unconstitutional nonsense that is being used to distract from the gross incompetence or massive hypocritical malfeasance that began with Maxine Waters in 2016.

In the Biden context, Senate Majority Leader Chuck Schumer *"The theory that the Senate can't try former officials would amount to a constitutional get-out-of-jail-free card for any president who commits an impeachable offense."*

But, of course, Schumer was lying. If there was a real cause of action with regard to events on 6 January, if insurrection was the goal, if there were some form of sedition, any rational citizen would ask why "Citizen Trump" is not being charged under "18 U.S. Code § 2383 - Rebellion or insurrection." Find him guilty, sentence him, and then the 14th Amendment bars him from ever holding office again.

But Schumer knew the charge was bogus, and, as a graduate of Harvard College and Harvard Law School, he has sufficient legal background to know the impeachment was unconstitutional. And this was confirmed when Chief Justice John Roberts, declined to be the one presiding over the trial – a role Article 1, Section 3, Clause 6 mandates he take. But it is only mandated if the "Impeachment" is constitutionally lawful.

You read it before, read it again: *"The Senate shall have the sole Power to try all Impeachments. When sitting for that Purpose, they shall be on Oath or Affirmation. When the President of the United States is tried,* **the Chief Justice shall preside***: And no Person shall be convicted without the Concurrence of two thirds of the Members present."*

There is no flexibility – not when the Constitution explicitly utilizes the word *"SHALL."* And because the wording is based upon

"Shall", the Chief Justice cannot decline his role in a lawful hearing.

Destroying the Constitution for personal gain or power seems to be the driving force behind the House vote and now Schumer's Senate position. Ten Republicans chose to position themselves so that they too could tap the Swamp Denizen power acquisition.

There is a real challenge before the American Voter – are they willing to destroy the Constitution because one group, dominated by remaining members of the Silent Generation, seek its destruction?

Granted, they are not alone. We saw AOC jump on the anti-Constitution bandwagon when she decided to attack the Electoral College and was joined by the other members of "The Squad."

Then there is also the "Lincoln Project" and its movement to undermine the government and Constitution – knowing it can then turn on the Progressives and destroy them. In terms of Republican Christian values, the "Lincoln Project" has a curious aspect – it's founder, John Weaver, is either a bisexual or homosexual man who, apparently, sought to conceal his gayness through marriage to a woman and the fathering of children.

Interestingly, Political Consultant Karl Rove had the story or dirt on John Weaver back in 2004. If we look at the far-right and its supposed morality, we see a group whose tradition is opposed to the LGBTQ community. And yet, we have the "Lincoln Project" abandon the right to align with the liberal left-wing under the leadership of a man who, after decades of denial, finally came out of the clooset and stated: *The truth is that I'm gay. And that I have a wife and two kids who I love. My inability to reconcile those two truths has led to this agonizing place.*"

Thus, the "Lincoln Project" founder emerges as is a *deceiver of men*" who is more at home with the likes of Schiff and Nadler who proclaimed their "overwhelming evidence" of nothing – apart from the blatant lie that it pertained to something meaningful. Now, the lies are followed up by claims of "sedition" and are presented in an unconstitutional context aimed at creating an authoritarian regime that would put nations like Iran to shame.

If we look at the way the Covid-19 pandemic experience has been handled, we see something designed to promoted the Asian practice of wearing masks during cold and flu season. And as more is learned about Covid and the Coronavirus, the science seems to indicate it is a variation on the common cold – but one that, as the

CDC weekly data chart (in Chapter 3) showed, is a culling virus that is being credited for common causes of deaths that would otherwise have occurred in the same time period.

Based on the global reaction, in April 2020, Professor Barry Eichengreen, a University of California professor of economics, had no difficulty challenging President Trump's belief that, once Covid-19 was contained, the economy would return to where it had been.

The vast majority of nations dominated by European ancestry have taken a self-destructive path. China, the supposed nation of origin, has seen a 2.3% economic growth while the Western nations have seen contractions approaching 10%.

There is a difference between East and West. How we codify it is affected by what we are inclined to blame for social failures. In reality, the East, as represented by China, is mercantile. In the world of the anti-Semite, this trait is also common to Jewish tradition as if it was a negative. But, as we know, it is a Biblical mandate that defines the role of the merchant and the supporter of the scholar – which is also the traditional Chinese mandate.

The West has a history of conquest, of violence, of slavery, of inflicting harm while also exuding creativity and growth – even while it attempts to suppress wisdom, knowledge and understanding. We can look to America – the United States – as a refuge for the creative and all who were escaping the oppression that defined Europe. At the same time, it also attracted the oppressors and that dual reality is now being resolved.

With the 58th Presidential Inauguration, the nation stepped into a new era – one of a major transition defining the nature of the country for the next 57 quadrennial cycles. The problem being that few powerful states manage to survive 62 quadrennial cycles – which means, if we count from the Revolution, 2024 is the death year for the United States.

If we choose to count from Thursday, 30 April 1789, the first Presidential Inauguration, than we have until 2037 – if we accept a Biblical doctrine which has shaped most of European and American history since the time of Roman domination over Israel, there is an apocalyptic World War Three is due in 2035. At least that is the year determined by Sir Isaac Newton's analysis of Revelation, and the year confirmed – using a different method of calculation of that text, as presented in my 2014 book, *"Biblical Prophecy: Are we in the*

Revelation Era".

Greenhouse gases, Climate Change, the ASAP need for a net-zero carbon footprint that many say they wish to achieve by 2050, but which we need to achieve much sooner, will cause a level of global warming that will spawn mass migrations, political conflicts and ultimately war. The year 2035 is not irrational, nor should it be dismissed as mysticism or superstition.

That the ancients used a cyclical projection is not a function of some religious mystical stupidity. As I showed in the calculation method used in *"Biblical Prophecy,"* since we have no starting day for the 2,000-year period, we can take several meaningful days and see where the cycles come together. Coincidently, the Roman era symbol for the Germanic tribes was a White Horse and 1931, saw the rise of Hitler to a position of power in the German Reich. And when we start there, the dates and symbolic assertions held together.

We can dismiss many things, but we are told that a third of all life will die in this period – are we going to argue that there are no mass extinctions being caused by Climate Change? Are we going to argue that the combination of a Baby-Bust and the death of the Baby-Boomer population will not significantly reduce the human population by the year 2050?

Now we are faced with a Culling Virus – not a indiscriminate Black Plague or 1918 Influenza that kills the otherwise healthy, but a stupid little virus that only amplifies already pre-existing medical conditions in a way that expedites the death of the elderly – cleanses the population of the sickly Silent and Baby-Boomer generations.

CHAPTER EIGHT – Games
"The Senate trial would therefore begin after President Trump's term has expired..."
~ Memo statement by Senator Mitch McConnell

On 13 April 2020, with over 10,000 dead, Governor Cuomo declared *"The worst is over"* for New York State. However, February 2021 saw the number of New York dead surpass 43,350.

On the monetary side, Cuomo oversaw the creation of a $52 million temporary hospital in Queens. That was $52 million spent to treat 79 patients while paying its doctors as much as $732 an hour during the month it was operating.

That form fiscal responsibility explains why the monied elite are once again exiting New York – in the 1950s, it was called "White Flight" related to the influx of Puerto Ricans and the new generation of former soldiers seeking home ownership. But now it is the same effect that Arthur Laffer pointed to in England as the basis for his "Laffer Curve" which then became a cornerstone of President Ronald Reagan's economic policy.

Reagan's tax reduction policies became the foundation of the Republican taxation agenda. The rich were given ways to avoid the taxes, and the average citizen was given the burden of supporting the government. Every plantation relied on its slaves while the masters wasted money and eventually went broke.

The problem that arose, as discussed earlier in this series, is that there is a point on the "Laffer Taxation Curve" where the taxes are actually too low and cause deficits which will ultimately serve to undermine the national economy.

Curiously, people really do not mind paying taxes – if the process is simple and they can identify a benefit they will receive. It is – again as mentioned previously in this series – the basis for the original 1870 creation of Social Security in Germany. Social Security is a pension that people will happily fund; it is old age security and a lottery. The lottery aspect is that they assume they will be alive to collect. In 1870, the retirement age in Germany was 65 and the life expectancy was 40.

In the modern age, Social Security is in trouble because the income level for contributions is only a fraction of earned money –

the cutoff omits those who are in or above the upper middle class.

The rule is simple, let the slaves pay for supporting the slaves.

The slave labor provides the basic housing for the slaves and the masters live in the mansion that is also paid for by slave labor.

The game never changed. Everything is the same, they just change the name and order of magnitude. When Social Security was first introduced, it was a tax that people would happily pay. The vast majority of those who paid for it were not expected to live long enough to collect. Because they would not be needing the money in the future, it became money that the government could spend.

Social Security was a lottery that was won by any who lived beyond the age of 65. And when the demographics change, when life expectancies increased and the average person was living long enough to collect, rather than increase the amount the wealthy paid, Congress raised the "full benefit" retirement age. We hear about the system being insolvent. But, it wouldn't be, if all earned income was subject to contributions – in 2021, those earning $142,800 or more will only contribute $8,853.60 a year to Social Security, while the rest of the workers will contribute 6.2% of their earnings.

With a median income of $68,703 and an average income of $97,973, it is clear the numbers are skewed to exempt high earning households from any meaningful contribution.

When we look at the promise versus the actual benefit, we see that the promise of a dignified retirement was a lie. Those on Social Security need secondary resources or must rely on a public assistance supplement to their monthly check. Of course, if they accept the supplement, they are attacked for being on welfare, for needing LIHEAP, SNAP, or any number of other programs whose cost should have been covered by the retirement income they paid for.

Now enter Covid-19 and the need to provide a stimulus that would keep the economy functioning. A one-time check for $1,200 that is followed by $600 and Biden promising $2,000 – only to be seen to lie when he reduces it to $1,400, the equivalent of one weekly median income paycheck. One week's income to makeup for being denied the right to work for nearly a year – that seems fair. At least it does to the overlords whose incomes have only increased.

Because he needs to hold his Progressive support base, Biden is now looking at a $15/hour minimum wage. Under Obama-Biden, that wage saw one increase, to the current $7.25/hour, and that didn't even adjust for the real costs covered by working.

If, as Bernie sanders does, we look back to 1965 and its $1.25 minimum wage, we can see the reality.

In 1965, it was possible to both work while paying your way through college. If we use New York City as a baseline, A Brooklyn Heights apartment that now costs several thousand a month – after you buy it – could be rented for $75 a month; the cost of a subway ride to work or school was $0.15 and gasoline was three gallons for a dollar.

Forget about the "basket" used for inflation and focus on the real cost of getting to and from a job. Back then, it was cheaper to own a motorcycle ($600 brand new) than ride the subway. But let's look just at the basic cost of going to work by subway.

In 1965, you made $1.25 and pay $0.15 to get to the job. In 2021 a subway ride costs $2.75 – to spend the same percentage of an hour's wage, you need to earn $22.92/hour. And if you drove to work, with the price of gas at $2.35/gallon, you could get by making $8.90/hour.

But that ignores the fact that, in 1965, a new top-of-the-line BMW was about $3,500 and, in 2021, it would be reasonable to pay $45,500; that means a minimum wage of $16.25 would make the two cars equally unaffordable. If you can find a car model that was made in 1965 and is still produced today – use that. Then, we can get fancy and factor in insurance, parking, and other annual routine costs like registration and inspections.

We tend to ignore that fact that, to earn a living, you need to go to your place of employment. With the Covid-19 pandemic, we know that remote working has begun to emerge and changes the cost dynamics for upper income workers. The average Walmart associate still needs to show up every day.

The system is geared to favor the upper income workers – it is their income that really keeps pace with inflation and changes in *their* basic daily costs. If the cost of a three martini lunch goes up, the tax deduction value to the company increases. There is no effect on the income of the executive drinking those martinis.

If we think about it, that costly three martini lunch – along with every other "deductible business meal" – actually enhances the income for the executive. The average person doesn't think about that reality, but it is, nevertheless, reality. If you eat out, you do not eat at home – so the cost of eating at home ... energy to refrigerate and then cook the food, the time cost for shopping and cooking, are all removed. Those who were single adults in the 1970s might recall the numerous articles that detailed how much cheaper it was to eat out than eat at home. And, if you can deduct the eating out as a business expense, not only is it even cheaper, but the food selection is far superior.

The system is designed to enrich the rich, while ensuring that slaves pay the cost.

Raise the minimum wage to $15. That is not going to adjust for day-to-day cost inflation imposed on minimum wage workers.

Is it going to increase the cost of some goods or services? It might. But the true current cost of those services includes public assistance and depleted health that has made those minimum wage workers the hub for the pandemic.

If the goal were to keep costs low, the first thing that would happen is the tax system would become a flat rate system where the full cost is carried by those making above the median wage.

Those making below the median wage will still be paying sales and property taxes. And, if back in school, you had a good civics teacher, you would know that the founding fathers envisioned a nation where property taxes carried the cost of government. In modern society, that would mean the Corporations or employers would be paying the taxes that support the huge military budget and pay the salaries of those who sit in Congress playing petty vindictive politics rather than doing the job of representing their constituents and promoting the best interests of the nation.

An example of the misrepresentation can be seen in both the words and actions of House Speaker Nancy Pelosi. Just before the announcement of Biden's actions favoring Tesla, Pelosi's husband invested heavily in Tesla stock – that's insider trading; privileged knowledge of information being used for personal profit.

Looking back to 14 June 2018, we find video of Pelosi inciting riots – or pondering why they aren't happening – when she said: "*I Just Don't Even Know Why There Aren't Uprisings All Over The Country. Maybe there will be.*"

At the time, the focus of her comment was blaming Trump for the Obama-Biden era policy of separating children from the parents at the border. Supposedly, because Trump continued what was an Obama-era policy he was immoral. Of course, she was silent when Obama initiated it and clearly was proud of the fact it had reduced the number of illegal crossings. But Pelosi is pro-open borders, and has held that position since the Reagan era – when Ronald Reagan promoted open borders and amnesty for all who violated American immigration laws.

On 17 August 2020, Representative Ayanna Pressley was on MSNBC and proud to say *"There needs to be unrest in the streets for as long as there is unrest in our lives."* She was calling for riots of the type that happened on 6 January 2021.

Obviously we are looking at people who have no regard for rules or the law. We can see the blatant dis regard in Pelosi's actions – she implements a metal detector screening policy, fines GOP members if they disregard it, then openly disregards it. Pelosi is "above the law" – laws and policies do not apply to her or any in her sphere of influence.

As we've seen in previous editions of this series, Pelosi was happy to impeach Trump for honoring a 1998 Clinton-Ukraine treaty for the sharing of investigation information. That is, she, along with her criminal ilk, held it to be an impeachable offense for a President to honor a decades old Democratic Administration treaty.

And what was he charged with? Supposedly he was entering into a *"Quid Pro Quo"* because he wanted relevant data on a Ukraine investigation into criminal activities that seemed to involve Joseph Biden – who, at an international forum, actually sat on the stage and bragged about having used a *"Quid Pro Quo"* involving taxpayer money to have a Ukrainian Prosecutor General fired because he was investigating the firm Hunter Biden worked for.

But Joe Biden is now President and, like Pelosi, is above the law. More important, because his Vice President is neither a POTUS Cousin nor descendant of the 4-Sisters, Biden cannot be removed without the nation falling.

Now we have a second Impeachment that is unconstitutional. On it's face, an action intended to remove a sitting President is being used to attack a former President. Plus we have the matter of who shall preside over a lawful impeachment – the Chief Justice of the Supreme Court, who declined the role, apparently because it was unconstitutional and therefore he had no obligation to preside.

And how was the House impeachment hearing conducted?

In the words of Louisiana Senator Bill Cassidy, we saw how the rule of law and due process were discarded, *"The president wasn't there. He wasn't allowed counsel. They didn't amass evidence. In five hours, they kind of judged, and boom, he's impeached. Now, I'm told that under the Watergate, under the Clinton impeachments, there were truckloads of information. Here, there was a video. There was no process. I mean, it's almost like, you know, if it happened in the Soviet Union, you would've called it a show trial."*

There was a video? And, compared to Pelosi calling for mob violence style unrest in the streets, what did it show Donald Trump saying?

It showed him telling those at the conventional "1963 March of Washington" style gathering: *"I know that everyone here will soon be marching over to the Capitol building to peacefully and patriotically make your voices heard."*

When we look at the riot, it was the type of unrest Pelosi had envisioned; it was planned well in advance as a broad attack on both the Democratic and Republican members of Congress. It involved the planting of pipe-bombs and other actions that could not have happened if they were instigated through the words of President Trump that would be said a mile away and a half-hour or so after the riot had begun.

We had the dishonest House Manager Adam Schiff asserting *"a real sense of urgency because the president had just incited a mob that attacked the Capitol and killed, resulted in the deaths of five people."*

As a attorney, Adam Schiff should be disbarred and forbidden to hold elective office after demonstrating gross incompetence and stupidity related to his inability to read the Constitution and show a basic understanding of impeachment as an action for the removal of a sitting president – not one already removed by a general election.

Of course, in the ideal modern world, the Democrats plus 17 Republicans will comprise the necessary 67 votes to convict and the history books will record Donald John Trump as the first American President to be successfully impeached.

Were Trump guilty of the alleged sedition or any other level of nonsensical assertions, the Administration could simply order the

Attorney General to prosecute him for those crimes. But the true intent is to distract the public from the tax games that are or will be played under the guise of addressing the economic concerns of the pandemic.

Remember that this is not a court of law, there is no "burden or standard of proof" to be imposed on Senators who are both judge and jury. There are no conventional or other rules of evidence and the punishment is political with a verdict that cannot be appealed.

What is being proclaimed is not some real crime, high crime, or even a misdemeanor crime. What is being proclaimed is that the Swamp Denizens see Trump as a very real treat. They cannot find an honest means of defeating him and are well aware that they will not have a viable candidate in 2024.

While a Tulsi Gabbard could easily win, there is no possible way that they will want an intelligent and moral female – one who is also a military officer – to be in charge and in a position of power that would cripple their dishonest behavior.

But, in February 2021, the goal was to distort and disrupt.

The Democratic managers asserted "*The House denies each and every allegation in the answer that denies the acts, knowledge, intent, or wrongful conduct charged against President Trump. The House states that each and every allegation in the article of impeachment is true, and that any affirmative defenses and legal defenses set forth in the answer are wholly without merit.*"

It was the ideal "Lawyer's Lie" – without any sign of honesty or truth that might serve as camouflage – which then transformed into a "Lawyer's Lie" by asserting : "*The House further states that the article of impeachment properly alleges an impeachable offense under the Constitution, is not subject to a motion to dismiss.*"

The Constitution is clear. Impeachment is to remove a sitting President. There is no constitutional basis for attacking a former President through the impeachment process. If – per the House lie – there was "wrongful conduct," that conduct is subject to the Court to review and adjudicate.

The dishonesty extends to House Managers seeking to use the Senate impeachment trial of Secretary of War William Belknap in 1876. Problem being, a Secretary of War is not a President and the act of resigning to avoid Congressional action is not the same as an election that achieves the stated purpose of impeachment.

Moreover, we have an explicit assertion in Article 1, Section 3, Clause 6: *"When the President of the United States is tried, the Chief Justice shall preside."* If the Chief Justice is not presiding, it is indisputable – the impeachment process is unconstitutional. That violation of the Constitution, the end to the rule of law, is what the Swamp Denizens {House Managers} are seeking.

Former President Trump's lawyers made their position clear: "*The article of impeachment presented by the House is unconstitutional for a variety of reasons, any of which alone would be grounds for immediate dismissal. Taken together, they demonstrate conclusively that indulging House Democrats hunger for this political theater is a danger to our republic, democracy and the rights that we hold dear.*"

Having said that, the House managers repeated their song from the first impeachment – the evidence "*is overwhelming.*" It is so "*overwhelming*" that they could not present it before the House voted to impeach and they will need to take weeks or months to find and present it for the Senate trial – or they will continue to yell that it is "*overwhelming*" and be too overwhelmed by it to present it.

It doesn't matter, our magic number – 57 – has appeared as the percentage of Americans who want Trump convicted.

It appears to be the percentage of Americans who would be happy to see the rule of law destroyed because they have such a clear image of *The Emperor's New Clothes* that nothing will dissuade them.

According to the House Managers, Trump's "incitement of insurrection against the United States government" is clear. Maybe not as clear as Nancy Pelosi's was in 2018 or Pressley's call for unrest in the streets – but then, Trump's insurrection call was predicated on "*peacefully and patriotically make your voices heard*" and not the distant mob violence condoned by Pelosi and Pressley.

It is also interesting to note that, in a procedural vote that the MSM decided was to be presented as a vote on the Constitutionality of the Senate Trial, our number 56 emerged as the number of votes to proceed with the trial – 50 Democrats and 6 Republicans voted to follow the Senate Rules.

In January, Senator Bill Cassidy (R-La.) Had voted to dismiss the Impeachment. But when it came to honoring a constitutional procedural mandate, he joined with Senators Susan Collins (Maine),

Mitt Romney (Utah), Ben Sasse (Neb.), Pat Toomey (Pa.) and Lisa Murkowski (Alaska) to set aside the misstated issue.

Senator Josh Hawley (R-MO), asserted that the Constitution does not support the trial. But when he asserted: "*The Constitution doesn't allow it. ... The Constitution doesn't give the Senate the power to try and convict private citizens. I mean, it just doesn't,*" he was engaged in a classic form of Lawyer's Lie that mixes "apples and oranges."

He was correct. The Senate cannot place a private citizen on trial for an alleged crime or misdemeanor. But the Senate must hear the evidence or relevant basis for a House indictment of a "*Sitting President*" – doesn't matter if they are still in office or, even, alive.

There are procedures. The constitution is explicit about what constitutes a lawful impeachment trial. And it is there that we see "*The Constitution doesn't allow it.*"

While Hawley was wrong in his premise, he was correct in the true goal being promoted by Swamp Denizens seeking to undermine the United States Constitution and *due process*: "*every time we have a switch in party, you're going to see now the majority party coming in and saying let's try the ex-president.*"

This outcome is what we see after a political or military coup – it provides the basis for using a guillotine on the replaced nobility. In the case of America, on any who are both POTUS COUSINS and descendants of the 4-Sisters. A beauty of the guillotine is that it is a violent show that distracts people from the reality of their lives for at least a decade – a decade defined by a violent transition into some form of dictatorial existence.

Representative Joe Neguse (D-Colo.), in his capacity as a House manager, played the Lawyer's Lie game by asserting: "*You don't need to be a constitutional scholar to know the argument President Trump asks you to adopt is not just wrong, it's dangerous. ... There is no January exception to the impeachment power, that presidents can't commit grave offenses in their final days and escape any congressional response.*"

But nobody argued a "*January exception.*" There was the idea that the Constitution states Impeachment only applies to "*THE*" President and not a former President who has been legally voted out of office.

The House voted the Articles of Impeachment while Trump

as *"THE"* President – and that makes their vote legally binding on the Senate. That this is beyond the comprehension of a 36-year-old Californian who is a son of immigrants and weirdly fixated on the calendar rather than the Constitution and Congressional rules – well that is to be expected.

In explaining her vote, Senator Murkowski stated the real issue in a rather clearly: *"The vote today was not about President Trump. It was about the Senate retaining jurisdiction to try a former official who was impeached while in office for acts done while in office."*

The impeachment was brought while Trump was President; accordingly, we have the matter as phrased in a memo by Senate Majority Leader, Mitch McConnell: *"The Senate impeachment rules provide that at 1pm the day after the [House Impeachment] Managers exhibit the articles before the Senate, the Senate must proceed to their consideration. ... The Senate trial would therefore begin after President Trump's term has expired — either one hour after its expiration on January 20, or twenty-five hours after its expiration on January 21."*

The fact that the Senate composition and leadership changed did not alter the legal obligation to hear the charges. However, there remains the problem that the Constitution refers to an Impeachment without relevance to any change in status of the accused, or calendar month in which *"Managers exhibit the articles before the Senate."*

Representative Neguse has clearly demonstrated he either lacks the knowledge and qualification to comprehend the procedural process or, he his intentionally being blatantly dishonest and has been engaged to sell people on the beauty of *"The Emperor's New Clothes."*

Pelosi and her Swamp Denizens intentionally brought a false complaint against President Donald John Trump. And, by doing so they added a final consistency of the focus phase to the impeachment they have sought since the 2016 election results were announced.

The procedural vote did not deal with a key issue – for the trial to be Constitutional, the Chief Justice MUST preside. But, since this is a political show trial, those Republican Senators who voted to support procedure were correct. But Mitch McConnell can also be seen as correct in opposing the procedural continuity in the absence of the Chief Justice presiding.

Part of the game is to provide a distraction from the reality of the pandemic and the economic games being played by the House of Representative.

One of the House Managers was Eric Swalwell, a member of House Intelligence Committee who had been implicated as a long-time connection for an alleged Chinese Spy. In that context, House Minority Leader Kevin McCarthy was on record saying: *"The Intel committee is different than any other committee. It is the most difficult committee to get on. It's only selected by the leaders of both parties. He got on as a sophomore. How could he do that? They were in the minority at the time, not very many seats. He got on as a sophomore and now, he says, that Nancy Pelosi and Adam Schiff knew of it. This is a national security threat. ... And now we have Eric Swalwell whose been swindled by the Chinese but what's even more interesting here is why did he attack the American Director of Intelligence John Ratcliffe's report, talking about the expansion of China spying throughout?...This man should not be in the Intel committee."*

Obviously, Trump opposed China's influence and moves to dominate the global mercantile platform that defines the basis of America's strength and importance of the dollar as the global reserve currency.

There is an interesting pattern. A Manchurian Candidate in the Oval Office, and a possible Manchurian agent assisting with the prosecution of a former President who is deemed a serious threat to the Swamp Denizens.

As of the second day of the Senate Trial, we know 200 people who were charged in connection to the riot. Will House Managers make any attempt at all to draw a straight line between them and President Trump?

We know the riot was well planned and the House Judiciary Committee wants to hold Trump accountable – but, can he really be held accountable for the actions of others...actions done without his knowledge or approval? Actions which are full consistent with those Pelosi et al called for over a period spanning several years.

Not that it matters. We start with economics affecting every citizen and get distracted by the details and legality of the current historically unique impeachment process. That was the idea.

CHAPTER NINE – Surf's Up

"We are not saying we predict that coal will be phased out. What we are saying is, this is now a splendid opportunity, and it would be good if energy ministers and finance ministers around the globe will take advantage of the situation." ~ Ottmar Edenhofer, director Potsdam Institute

The Constitution demands obedience through its simple and explicit construction. Attach the words President and Impeachment and you dictate the procedure. Unless the Constitution asserts a different procedure for a former President, then Article 1, Section 3, Clause 6 controls the events. But the Constitution does make it clear that impeachment is for the removal from office of a sitting President, not the preventing of a former President from running again.

Initiate impeachment while the President is in office and you have until their lawful term expires to complete the process – if the individual submits a resignation, they have submitted a defacto admission of guilt and the process can continue until the normal end of their term. But, lawful transfer of power through an Election and the Inauguration of their successor does end the impeachment. Iof there is a legitimate crime, the matter must then, in accordance with the Constitution, go to the criminal courts.

The fact that the House Managers are dishonest and yell they have *"Overwhelming Evidence"* does not constitute any legitimate basis for either an impeachment of prosecution. And when that alleged evidence is shown, by a failure to detail it in the proceedings, not to exist, the House Managers should be removed from office and denied any right to hold office or practice law.

On Tuesday, 9 February, a piece in the Boston Globe asserted that *"The Constitution doesn't shield Trump from accountability. It demands it."* And that is true.

But, the Constitution and the heart of any Democratic process also demands that those who lie and present false witness through the assertion of non-existent *"Overwhelming Evidence"* must also be held accountable to the fullest extent of a lawful political process.

President Trump was first impeached for invoking a 1998 information sharing Treaty with the Ukraine – after Joseph Biden bragged of using federal money as part of a *Quid Pro Quo* blackmail scheme to remove a Prosecutor General engaged in investigating Ukraine corruption involving a firm that had paid Hunter Biden and his partner an exorbitant amount to lobby for them in Washington. In an interview, Hunter even admitted that much of his income was directly related to the "Biden name" and the influence wielded by his father.

According to Chuck Cooper, a conservative attorney quoted in the article, *"Given that the Constitution permits the Senate to impose the penalty of permanent disqualification only on former officeholders, it defies logic to suggest that the Senate is prohibited from trying and convicting former officeholders."*

Of course, Cooper's statement constitutes a "Lawyer's Lie."

After a lawful impeachment, conviction, and removal from office prior to the natural expiration of their term, there impeached individual is also denied the right to ever again hold an office that is tied to moral stature – the conviction having established that they are untrustworthy and, in the context of holding a position of moral leadership, immoral.

Nothing in the Constitution asserts the right of the House or Senate to impeach a private citizen or former office holder. If they are guilty of crimes, the Criminal Court must so determine, and with that determination, other statutes allow disqualification. But, if that is the law, than anyone who has served time in Prison for a felony or action which is unlawful by Federal Law must also be prohibited from holding an office of prestige, honor, or power.

Members of the House and Senate swore an oath to *"defend the Constitution of the United States against all enemies, foreign and domestic."* But, as of 9 February, the world was witness to the effect of a partisan disregard for that oath and persistent lies about there being *"Overwhelming Evidence"* in a matter where, for the second time, the complainants were unable to present any evidence.

As stated, the premise of the first impeachment was that the President honored his oath of office and invoked a valid treaty after a former public official openly confessed to blackmailing a foreign government while in office.

Now we see the second impeachment – brought after a lawful election that removed the President effective on a data-certain (the Inauguration of his successor) and once again we see the crime is the core of Democracy reminding voters that they have a right to, in a peaceful orderly manner, let their voices be heard by those they elected to represent them.

Granted, there remains the persistent question as to exactly how lawful the election was. And it is important to note that those promoting silencing people on that issue are the same ones who have consistently promoted gerrymandering as a means of manipulating elections.

How honest are these people?

In the Georgia election, voters were told that, if they elected the Democratic candidates they would receive pandemic hardship checks in the amount of $2,000 – candidate Joseph Biden explicitly stated he would immediately push for the $2,000 checks. We note that this was also the amount President Trump stated he wanted and the Congress seemed to oppose – and, as of 9 February, are doing all in their power to reduce to $1,400 while also disqualifying many who received the earlier $600 checks.

Those involved with the lies and deceptions might be calling themselves Democrats, but they would be better identified as *DINO* – not just dinosaurs in there positions and politics for power, but as *Democrats In Name Only* when it comes to the Progressive policies introduced by Franklin Delano Roosevelt.

Having gotten this far in the series, and as we come to an end which will be marked by the anticipated 2nd impeachment acquittal of Donald John Trump, readers should keep in mind we have been surfing the events from under the curve, not racing ahead of it as my books on prophecy and patterns normally do, but rather reacting as the wave folds in on us.

To some it might seem confusing. But, to those who read this series with the benefit of hindsight that comes with a few decades of history between the events and the evaluation, the series should grant some level of insight to the reality that will have brought them to where they are – if the prophecy is correct, that means a major war, around 2035, that is accompanied by a 49th President, and the realization that the world they occupy has a third less species than the world in which this is being written. There is even the likelihood that the peak human population will have passed and they are living in a time when the population has been reduced by a third of that peak number.

We are riding a surfboard through a period of historic change and the wave is folding in – we stand in the barrel or tube – driving events, and we need to maintain both balance and momentum with the focus on not wiping out.

There is the wave propelling us that is the media attention; there is a tide beneath the water's surface; there are smaller waves, wind chop, attempting to bring us down. There are also the breezes and winds of change we will feel when we exit our sheltered position under the crushing wave that defines the tunnel.

Waves break from left and right in an effort to disorient us – combative politics, a pandemic, Climate Change, militaristic regimes seeking to exploit the capabilities of all-out nuclear destruction and devastation, or simply mercantile powers looking to control markets.

Curiously, things we fear could be our greatest allies or best friends.

The growth of humanity has warmed the planet and change the ecosystem that spawned many species who have outlived their purpose. Land that was once too cold to be useful has now defrosted and will soon become quality farmland. The snows that buried us are now mild storms accompanied by extensive rain – the water that has evaporated comes back down in a form that is clean and fresh.

Climate change affected by coal emitted of greenhouse gases has been affected by the pandemic. In the days of Charles Dickens and his "Bah Humbug" Scrooge, coal as polluting the air in cities and the polluting was a poison that spawned lung diseases and weakened the immune systems as diseases like tuberculosis emerged.

Now we have a culling virus – coronavirus – that chooses as its target those who are already sickly. In New York City, a third of the dead were in nursing homes where they required 24-hour care and attention.

That evil pandemic! One of its effects has been to change our behavior in a way that has produced cleaner air. In terms of Dickens' coal, during the pandemic, its use has dropped significantly and with it the greenhouse gas focus of the Paris Climate Accord. Electricity use has changed – we use more while using less.

The simple things powered by electric are becoming more efficient – those incandescent bulb known to the Silent and Baby-Boomers are being replaced with LED and the computers that once occupied thousands of square feet and required their own HVAC systems to keep them at a steady temperature are gone – in their place are cellphones that are actually far more powerful.

Some of us even welcome the little bit of heat cast off by our laptop or tablet. Soon we will have electric cars and the reliance of oil will decrease – much to the chagrin of the OPEC nations. Those vehicles will, in rural areas be charged by the same solar or wind that will be powering the average rural home and business.

Of course the fun of surfing through this period is that nobody cares about the changes that are happening. There is a faction calling for change – but offing nothing to encourage and expedite it – and those who are in total denial of what is happening...even while they are part of the change being made.

But the idea behind the Impeachment is to avoid change. It is a distraction brought about by those who are too incompetent to survive outside of politics.

Senators are sworn in as jurors, the experience of having been forced to flee for safety recounted in graphic videos recorded that day makes the jurors the witnesses. So why call witnesses?

 After all, the jurors have their experience to draw upon – but that experience is the alleged aftermath of the crime which was the speech and not the personal experience. Thus the witness witnessed nothing of significance and the first thing you do is show is show them a video of what they might have experienced. But, unless they are actually in the video, they did not experience it.

Where are the witnesses whose experience was derived from actions planned, in detail, days or weeks before the speech?

The liars or has-been lawyers wish to blame the actions on the speech, and not those who planned the deed – those who planned it were onsite planting pipe bombs in the hours before the speech was given. Are we to believe they heard the speech and traveled back in time to do their evil deeds?

By some timelines, the rioters were doing their damage well before Trump's call for them to peacefully let their voices be heard.

As for Trump, he declined to testify -- the speech speaks for itself -- so he'll be content watch the kangaroo court circus from his Mar-a-Lago club in Florida.

Trump has already made history.

He's the first sitting President to be impeached twice for high crimes and misdemeanors while in office, the first president to face a Senate trial after being voted out of office, and, because he legally left office as the result of an Election in which he received a record number of votes, the first to have his trial conducted in deliberate breach of Article 1, Section 3, Clause 6 of the Constitution.

Trump was being given extended access to the reality of the "*bully pulpit*" described in the expression coined by President Teddy Roosevelt. But Donald John Trump is somewhat different in that he carries his own "*bully pulpit*" – so much so that CNN rating dropped 44% after the Inauguration.

A verdict in favor of Trump would grant him the opportunity to repeat the separate 2nd election achieved by Glover Cleveland – it would enhance his place in the history books.

Were Trump convicted, it would not be a defeat. Does anyone really he wants to experience four more years of attacks like those that marked his first four? Does Melania really want to deal with the role of First Lady a second time? Does either want to see Baron deal with being a college student first child?

On 18 November 2019, Trump had cheered impeachment. At the time he said, "*Impeachment? I'm for it. Great idea. Best idea, maybe ever. [I'm] getting kinda sick of all this winning anyway. … Sure, why not. Impeach me. I love it. Whatever. Now I'm gonna go watch Joker again. Great film. What's that guy's name? Phoenix something. Bob Phoenix, that's it. Tremendous actor – absolutely perfect.*"

Oh well, the actor's name isn't "Bob" it's Joaquin Phoenix, or, to be more accurate, Joaquin Rafael Bottom. He and his siblings all adopted the stage surname "Phoenix" – a mythical Greek creature that rises from the ashes of its predecessor. In modern mythology, it could be a regenerative *Dr. Who*. In any mythological context, it still seems a match for Trump's emerging mythology – which explains why he would welcome impeachment, or new ashes to emerge from.

Trump could easily profit from being allowed to continue to challenge those opposed to the nation's civic norms and traditions based on their lies about nonexistent "overwhelming evidence" – when the true evidence is that of their own misdeeds.

Ultimately, historians will declare the Swamp Denizens would have been far wiser to remain quiet and enjoy their electoral victory. But, had they done so, they would have lost their last opportunity to bring "the Great Experiment" to an end and with that action destroy the "*Shining City on the Hill*" foreseen in an 1630 sermon by John Winthrop that was adopted and repeated by Ronald Reagan.

America is exceptional. As Harvard historian Perry Miller is noted to have recognized when he resurrected Winthrop's "*city on the hill*" analogy, the exceptional nature dates to the emergence of those I identified as *Jonathon's POTUS Cousins* – the descendants of the 4-Sisters that the creative and most productive of every nation wanted to join. And until now, they still want to be part of America's great experiment.

But then, their actions are designed to fulfil Prophecy – the Prophecy of America's Destruction – and isn't that more fun? Isn't that what Russia, China, Iran, and so many others, want?

We can play with prophecy, with analogies, with a concept that was derived from the Bible – Matthew 5:14-17 "*You are the light of the world. A city set on a hill cannot be hidden. ... let your light shine before others, so that they may see your good works ... 'Do not think that I have come to abolish the Law or the Prophets; I have not come to abolish them but to fulfill them.'*"

Unfortunately the Swamp Denizens are devoted to abolishing the law and the nation.

The House was wise to ditch the previous House Managers and turn to a different group of destructive denizens.

This time out, we have a former professor of Constitutional Law at America University, Jamie Raskin, serving as lead manager. He makes a good presentation and is intelligent enough to avoid the constitutional issues where he'd be torn between conceding the trial, in the absence of the Chief Justice, is illegal, or acknowledge that you cannot try someone for inciting an action that was planned days or weeks before they spoke.

We have a five term Hispanic Congressman, Joaquin Castro – from Texas; a six term House member, David Cicilline; a two term member, Madeleine Dean; a thirteen term member, Diana DeGette; four term members, Ted Lieu and Stacey Plaskett. In all a cute team of lawyers who discovered they could make a better living in Congress – sucking the public tit – than they could by practicing law.

And with the Impeachment, they found a way to perpetrate the ultimate fraud – violating their oath of office by knowingly violating the Constitution. Specifically, NOT having the Chief Justice preside.

CHAPTER TEN – The [non] Case
"It is better to offer no excuse than a bad one."
~ George Washington

The case against Trump was predicated on his telling those at the rally *"I know that everyone here will soon be marching over to the Capitol building to peacefully and patriotically make your voices heard."*

Granted, Trump did use some descriptive rhetoric and, at one point, seven minutes and eleven seconds into the speech, the crowd shouted out it's support with the phrase: *"Fight for Trump! Fight for Trump! Fight for Trump!"*

We know he mentioned "fighting the House" – he specifically acknowledged those in the House of Representatives who were standing up to the dishonesty being perpetuated by Pelosi: *"We have great ones, Jim Jordan, and some of these guys. They're out there fighting the House. Guys are fighting, but it's incredible."*

Trump made it that, *"Republicans are constantly fighting like a boxer with his hands tied behind his back. It's like a boxer, and we want to be so nice. We want to be so respectful of everybody, including bad people."*

And, WOW! He took pride in the idea of being *"so respectful of everybody, including bad people,"* even after, a few years earlier, he had been attacked for declaring that, when Americans express their beliefs, there were "good people" among the bad.

Of course he described the fighting: *"But it used to be that they'd argue with me, I'd fight. So I'd fight, they'd fight. I'd fight, they'd fight. Boop-boop. You'd believe me, you'd believe them. Somebody comes out. They had their point of view, I had my point of view. But you'd have an argument. Now what they do is they go silent. It's called suppression. And that's what happens in a communist country."*

This is what the Constitution violating House Managers and Senate leader Schumer like to call insurrection – standing up for your opinion until the silence of the other party shows you have won. They then engage in fraudulent attacks.

In the case of the impeachment, even though it was irrational, it was lawful to bring an action prior to Biden's Inauguration and at a time when Trump was still the lawful President. Because the vote to impeach was lawful, the Senate was bound by law to address it.

However, the Senate would have been within it's legal right to declare the Articles of Impeachment moot – Constitutionally, the intent is to remove a sitting President prior to the natural expiration of their term in office.

Since Trump's term had ended, the Constitutional basis for the action no longer existed. If there had actually been a violation of law – be it a high crime or a high misdemeanor – the legal remedy falls to the Federal Court to adjudicate.

As noted throughout this book, #A1S3C6 of the Constitution is very clear on who presides over the impeachment of a President – the Chief Justice of the Supreme Court. That John Roberts declined and Schumer still proceeded with the farce indicates: 1. Roberts determined he had no Constitutional obligation to preside over what was clearly a fraudulent process in which the Constitutional purpose had been legally rendered moot. And, 2. That Chuck Schumer was willing to violate both the Constitution and his oath of office so as to conduct a shame trial based on an indictment rendered without due process or any evidentiary basis or support.

As the House Managers showed, all they could present was video of the riots – which clearly showed participants in body armor that proves prior planning – without any direct line to the President or anything he stated at the rally.

As observed by Senator Ted Cruz (R-Texas) on 10 February: *"The footage is horrific. They spent a great deal of time focusing on the horrific acts of violence that were played out by the criminals, but the language from the president doesn't come close to meeting the legal standard for incitement."*

The House Managers based their whole presentation on showing violence then connecting it to the rhetorical use of the word *"Fight."*

For context, on 21 May 2019, Joe Biden Tweeted, *"That's why I've spent my whole career fighting – and I will continue to fight – like hell so that no one ever has to make that walk again."* In its context, the resurrected quote was describing Biden's father walking up the stairs in the family home to tell them they were moving from Pennsylvania to Delaware so that he could continue to make a living.

So! Biden is going to *"fight – like hell"* to ensure no other families must relocate to a different state in order to survive. Yet, is Biden actively telling Congress to cease its unconstitutional activities and get down to the business of issuing the survival funds?

On 15 December 2020, Biden used "fight" in a tweet: *"Health care is -personal to me – and I'll always fight to ensure folks like Xiomara are protected and have access to the care they need."* So we know he will fight for health care but, apparently, he will not fight to honor the words of the Constitution as presented in #A1S3C6.

We have lead House Manager, Representative Jamie Raskin (D-Md.), who The NY Post pointed out had invoked *"the notion of combat to block Republican efforts to swiftly replace the late US Supreme Court Justice Ruth Bader Ginsburg following her death in September."*

He did so in the context of charging that, *"The GOP rush to replace Justice Ginsburg is all about destroying the Affordable Care Act, women's health care and reproductive freedom, and the voting rights and civil rights of the people. ... We must fight like hell to stop this assault on health care and the Constitution."* And, in terms that were echoed by Trump, Raskin stated *"This is our Democracy – fight for it."*

The Post went on to cite a 2019 Atlantic magazine interview in which Raskin had no problem asserting *"Let's hope for the best, be prepared for the worst, and go fight like hell for the Constitution."* But, as seen with his ignoring #A1S3C6, Raskin is no longer interested in fighting to uphold the Constitution – instead he has taken the position of a leader in the process of undermining it.

Does Raskin like to describe fighting? He did in 2017 when he asserted, *"We've got to wake up every day and fight like hell for liberal democracy, not just in Maryland, not just in the United States, but all over the world."*

Also in 2017, House Manager Ted Lieu (D-Calif) took Michelle Obama's, "When they go low, we go high," and stated, *"I like that. But I like better, 'when they go low, we fight back'."*

In 2018, in roughly the context Trump used it, House manager Joe Neguse (D-Colo.) Endorsed Kamala Harris by stating he was *"truly humbled to have the support of such a fearless leader as we fight to take back Congress."*

What the Impeachment has taught America, and the World, is that it should be viewed as criminal to "fight like hell" to have your voices heard by those who are paid to represent and protect you. We have learned they will violate the Constitution – even when the words are preceded by the legally inflexible "SHALL" as the mandate.

It is also curious that the videos chosen by House prosecutors show the individuals who were breaking through the Congressional windows were wearing bulletproof body armor.

That is not something that magically appears when a President says citizens should stand-up for their rights. And, as pointed out on Newsmax, by Trump adviser Jason Miller: *"It's not just President Trump that's being put on trial, it's the First Amendment. I wouldn't be surprised if our lawyers didn't get up tomorrow and say, stand up if any of the 100 senators here, stand up if you've never said the words 'fight' or 'fight like hell' on the campaign trail. Because guess what, every single senator in that room has said it."*

Clearly we have what appears to be an assault on freedom of speech. But that is an abstract issue – there is a line drawn at falsely *"yelling 'FIRE' in a crowded theater."* However, as the record shows, those who are accusing Trump have recently based their career on the encouragement of violence in the streets. With Kamala Harris, the current Vice President, we see a person who organizes bail for those who burn and pillage minority communities.

We can play with abstract destruction of Constitutional Rights, but #A1S3C6 is not an abstract. There is an explicit mandate that any impeachment trial of a President be presided over by the Chief Justice of the Supreme Court.

There is a law against issuance of a Bill of Attainder – *"an act of a legislature declaring a person, or a group of persons, guilty of some crime, and punishing them, often without a trial"* – which means the legislature cannot abandon due process and act as judge and jury to corrupt the rights of any person under its jurisdiction.

Four years of repeated false claims about the existence of some "Overwhelming evidence" that has never been produced is, in effect, the process that controls a Bill of Attainder. Under the rules applied to Trump, you are guilty until proved innocent and you are denied the right to prove your innocence because the evidence against you is never produced – only third party hearsay, baseless gossip, or some unattributed and unsubstantiated assertion is repeated as if it were fact.

The House managers have put on a fascist or communist show

trial based on videos of violence or disruption. They did not even attempt to make a connection between charged individuals and the President. At best with have a modern assertion of "*Will no one rid me of this meddlesome priest?*" And even there we see the planning was detailed long before the words were spoken.

On Friday, 12 February, the Defense began its presentation – if we turn to the Defense's pretrial brief, dated 8 February, we find, while #A1S3C6 is cited, they do not specifically address the absence of the Chief Justice of the Supreme Court. Since the document is pretrial, any facts existing at the time the trial actually began could not be claimed – so the omission was logical.

However they do point out: "*One might have been excused for thinking that the Democrats' fevered hatred for Citizen Trump and their 'Trump Derangement Syndrome' would have broken by now, seeing as he is no longer the President, and yet for the second time in just over a year the United States Senate is preparing to sit as a Court of Impeachment, but this time over a private citizen who is a former President.*"

As noted in earlier books in this series, '*Trump Derangement Syndrome*' appears to be a very real debilitating mental condition we find controlling current events – including the fact that many Biden voters suffered from 'TDS' to such a degree that they would not vote "for" a candidate, but were voting "against" Trump. And they were doing so in face of record high employment, record low minority and female unemployment, an absence of any new military conflict that was set against a background of record peace settlements between traditional enemies – all negotiated by the President's son-in-law.

Looking at the one they voted "for" we see a man who bragged about using federal money to blackmail a foreign government that was investigating his son's employer – the result being that the Chief Prosecutor was replaced by an engineer who had just been released for jail where he served time on a felony fraud conviction.

But "TDS" prevailed and so, in the brief, the Defense points out that there was a lack of firsthand information, and "*Of the 170 footnotes in the House Manager's Trial Memorandum, there were only three citations to affidavits of four law enforcement officers and they were merely referenced to support descriptions of what rioters were wearing and weapons that were found. The rest of the purported "facts" relied upon by these Constitutionally-charged prosecutors came from hearsay through the media .*"

The fact that there was documented weapons and military style body armor is sufficient evidence that the speech was not the driving motivator for the attack on Congress. And the fact the attack began concurrent with the opening words of the speech would also prove there was no linkage other than the attackers using the general focus on the speech as a distraction from their destructive agenda.

If a former President can be denied his constitutional rights based on hearsay, it follows that, henceforth, the rule of law shal be that any citizen can also be denied their rights – that we are to return to the days of the Salem Witch Trials when children can assert magic and magical powers exist in an adult and therefore the adult shall be put to death.

Or, can be subjected to a trial by water, whereby they are tied to a chair and submerged in water – if they die they are innocent, and if they remain alive are clearly a witch and therefore must be put to death.

The defense assert that the hour and fifteen minute speech was marked by the fact that it was, "*Notably absent from his speech was any reference to or encouragement of an insurrection, a riot, criminal action, or any acts of physical violence whatsoever. The only reference to force was in taking pride in his administration's creation of the Space Force.*"

The House Managers deem the crowd gathered to hear a speech from their President to be criminals, and not "*all the amazing patriots here today,*" seen by President Trump. It would appear that to be a patriot you must avoid attending a Presidential event – such events should be as devoid of an audience as those held by Joseph Biden.

When it comes to insurrection and overthrowing the lawful government the Defense Brief pointed out that, with less than two weeks before the Inauguration of Joseph R. Biden, "*Speaker Nancy Pelosi and Senate Democratic Leader Chuck Schumer called on Vice-President Pence to invoke the 25th Amendment concluding– without any investigation – that Mr. Trump incited the insurrection and continued to pose an imminent danger if he remained in office as President.*"

Think about that. Donald J. Trump had been in office for four years and with only two weeks left – after he had already established he was moving to Mar-A-Largo, Florida – Trump was such a threat that they wanted to make Mike Pence POTUS for the week or so before the swearing in of Biden.

As readers of this series know, Pence is not a POTUS Cousin, nor is he a descendant of the 4-Sisters, which means he would have broken the historic chain of Western or Global leadership dating back to the time of Charlemagne the Great. Whenever that chain is broken the nation involved falls into chaos and revolution driven destruction.

Since Pence declined, just as he declined Trump's request with regard to revisiting the Electoral College numbers, we are told that, *"Five days later, on January 11, 2020, House Democrats formally introduced House Resolution 24."* The next day Pelosi appointed the team of managers and the day after that, *"on January 13th, House Democrats completed the fastest presidential impeachment inquiry in history and adopted the Article of Impeachment over strong opposition and with zero due process afforded to Mr. Trump, against Constitutional requirements and centuries of practice."*

There was less than a week left in Trump's term. If he were planning an insurrection it would need to happen – or would have happened – and Pelosi, along with her supporters, would be dead. It is the nature of a violent insurrection to kill your enemies as quickly as possible. Sadly, Pelosi, Schumer, Schiff, Nadler, Waters, Raskin, etc, are all still alive – which provides clear evidence that there was no planned insurrection.

And, as the Defense pointed out, while *"The House Managers spent nearly thirty-five (35) of their seventy-seven (77) page Trial Memorandum rehashing stories written by the media of mischaracterized statements attributed to Mr. Trump many months before Mr. Trump addressed the crowd at the Ellipse in Washington, D.C. on January 6, 2021. Media reports and reporters' opinions are not facts and most assuredly are not facts that should form the basis for instituting the grave power of impeachment. More significantly, however, Mr. Trump was never charged in the Article of Impeachment with the claims made in these various reports."*

However, the fact that it was a rehash of stories in the media – stories initiated by those who would then cite the media accounts – that demonstrated the "wrap-up smear" technique Pelosi boasted of using (as cited in Chapter 6).

As Pelosi described or defined it: *"It's a diversionary tactic. It's a self-fulfilling prophesy, you demonize and then — the 'wrap-up smear.'''*

We see how it was used against Trump, when Pelosi tells us the technique begins when, *"You smear somebody with falsehoods and all the rest, and then you merchandise it. And then you (gesturing to the media) write it, and then they say, 'See, it's reported in the press that this, this, this, and this.' So they have that validation that the press reported the smear,..."*

Naturally, the House Managers incorporated the technique by filling 36 pages or 45% of their brief with baseless *'wrap-up smear'* data. They understand, as Pelosi effectively revealed, that the average person will see "The Emperor's New Clothes" they have been told to see. Not seeing it means they lack wisdom and are idiots. The wise see the wondrous beauty of the nonexistent garments.

Fifty percent of the Senate will, of course, see the non-existent garments and ignore all the Constitutional violations inherent in the breach of #A1S3C6, due process, etc. Liars create an 'illusion of truth' – for lawyers, it's the *"Lawyer's Lie"* which Johnny Depp's character, Captain Jack Sparrow, summarized with the statement, *"You lied to me by telling me the truth."*

If I tell you the truth in a manner you will not believe, I have lied to you without committing perjury. And isn't that the art of being the perfect politician? "I told you the truth. I'm not responsible for what you chose to hear."

Readers of this series are aware the technique was mentioned in Chapter 8 of book-10: "**POTUS FORTY *5.4.2 or 6.4.1* – The Pandemic President "Death of America"** (Sept 2020). But the same readers have repeated been told about the "Lawyer's Lie"; for me, it was basic learning, basic knowledge, because I was raised in a law firm and learned to read reading law books.

Repeat facts to drive them home, or repeat assertions to make them seem like facts and become a master of propaganda.

Nazi propagandist Joseph Goebbels is created with saying, *"Repeat a lie often enough and it becomes the truth."* It's a reality that defines human existence. We are all ware of this example: our year-one is the year when Jesus was born; as an infant, Jesus was taken to Egypt and had been there two years when Herod died, in the year 4BCE; thus, based on the lie we, as a culture, accept, Jesus had to have born at the age of seven and time traveled back so he could be in Egypt before Herod died.

Tell a lie, structure it so it is initially accepted, and then the lie becomes truth. It doesn't matter what the facts are or how irrational the exertion, before they will accept the reality, people will argue the lie and even bet their eternal souls on it.

The *"Illusion of Truth"* can help or hurt a society.

The birth of Jesus was an easier sale than explaining that year one was really the 198th Metonic node of the Hebrew calendar and was chosen because it allowed Passover and Easter to be brought into alignment.

However, as used by the Nazis, and those manipulating 'TDS' sufferers, the *"Illusion of Truth"* becomes a tool for undermining the social structure for personal gain or power.

As with the little boy in *"The Emperor's New Clothes"*, when the truth is pointed out, scientific studies show it will be accepted. It then becomes critical for the liars to perpetuate the lie and prevent the truth from emerging.

On Friday, 12 February, the Trump Defense Team spent two hours and 32 minutes of its allotted sixteen hours to rebut the House Manager presentation – which took about ten hours of their allotted time. Where the House showed the events without establishing any linear connection to Trump, the Defense presented a montage of videos depicting the Senators and some celebrities invoking "fight" as a focal point and energizing force in their rhetorical process.

There were no witnesses, there was no coherent structure that could denote direct responsibility or even foreknowledge of what was going on during the riot.

As with the first impeachment, there was no cited statutory reference, no explicitly charged crime, nothing that a prosecutor or judicial body could use as the base for asserting even a base crime – forget the idea of a "HIGH" crime. There was no investigation, no evidence, just a "rush to judgment" that concluded a process begun in November 2016.

On 12 Friday, the Chinese New Year rolled in – Celebrated at the second new moon following the Winter Solstice – the Year of the Ox replaced the Year of the Rat. It is a symbol of a creature who can be seen as industrious, reliable, honest and earnest – a creature that does things in the background and feels no need to be the center of attention. It is a year of endurance associated with the feminine, receptive Yin energy. And the impeachment vote will mark its start.

CHAPTER ELEVEN – 2nd Acquittal
"You furnish the pictures and I'll furnish the war."
~ William Randolph Hearst

In their pretrial brief, the Defense presented the legal meaning or definition of "shall" in this manner: *"Justice Scalia once wrote, when the word "shall" can reasonably be understood as mandatory, it ought to be taken that way. In 2007 the Supreme Court confirmed that 'The word `shall' generally indicates a command that admits of no discretion on the part of the person instructed to carry out the directive"); Black's Law Dictionary 1375 (6th ed. 1990) ("As used in statutes ... this word is generally imperative or mandatory")."*

The brief also defined why the case must be dismissed; *"The second reason a former President cannot be impeached follows logically from the first The purpose of impeachment is to remove someone from office, and unequivocally, this impeachment trial is not about removing someone from office, as Mr. Trump left office on January 20, 2021. He is now, both factually and legally, a private citizen."*

While I am simply stating the second reason provided, reality dictates that this is sufficient reason. You do not create an action to mandate that which has already been achieved under a different legal standard.

Perversely, acting to remove someone who has already been removed creates a non-judicial form of *"Double Jeopardy"* – the act of attempting to "punish" someone twice for the same act.

We know that, when there is a specified crime, impeachment for a "high" crime or misdemeanor is not deemed *"Double Jeopardy"* when that crime is later prosecuted by the judicial system.

The first is simply to remove over evidence of the appearance of the misuse of the office to commit a crime and the second is that actual action of prosecuting that crime. Impeachment is not evidence of complicity in a crime, it is based on overwhelming evidence of the appearance of principle action or complicity. Being impeached does not mean there will be a civil prosecution.

OJ Simpson was found innocent of murder – to a large degree because the car allegedly used in the crime was not at his home at the time of the crime or anytime thereafter until the following day – and a firsthand eyewitnesses established OJ was at home at the time the Bronco was missing and throughout the period when the murders were committed. That finding of innocence did not stop OJ from being sued and held responsible for millions in damages. Same basis but two very different results.

As with OJ, the media and Swamp denizens will persist in their attacks. Unlike OJ, the area is one of politics where the accusers must be and remain squeaky clean – when two pigs are fighting in the mud, the one the farmer turns one of them into bacon is the one who dies is the one whose death is deemed most profitable.

Of course, there could be a real profit in killing both – MSM is the one to make that determination about if and when each pig will be slaughtered. As mentioned below, Governor Cuomo was a pig to protect – in part because his brother is a CNN Commentator – but, with the anticipated 2nd impeachment trial outcome made official, that pig is going to the slaughter house.

After the 2nd acquittal, Republican strategist Alex Conant was on record saying, *"It's hard to imagine Republicans winning national elections without Trump supporters anytime soon. The party is facing a real Catch 22: it can't win with Trump but it's obvious it can't win without him either."*

Of course, it's a choice between "pig to slaughter" or "pig to reproduce." The Republicans win with serving to rally the troops in the same way he stole them from the Tea Party and Birthers. But it should be down without him on any ticket.

As has been stated throughout this book series, Trump is a P.T. Barnum, he's the penultimate intellectual showman before the great transition in 2040.

The media attacks him because they know that's the only way they'll attract his loyal followers and create the buzz that translates into an audience for advertisers. When he exited the Oval Office, CNN ratings fell by 44 percent – that indicates a significant revenue loss in a pandemic period that finds more people home watching TV than at anytime in previous years.

For now, Trump should not be a focal point for Republicans. They should allow the SWAMP DENIZENS to focus on the former President and devote their time to watching what his kids are doing. It's the kids, Don Jr, Eric, and Ivanka who will be defining the next decade of elections. All the while, Tiffany will be growing her family, honing her legal credentials, and then, when she and the family deem her ready, she will emerge as an unstoppable force.

The whole act to impeach was frivolity, an action of mindless, petty, vengeful frivolity intended to distract the public attention from the harm being done – and the Congressional failure to address the needs of the nation during this transitional era.

On 13 February, after a unanimous consent vote to allow both parties to submit unverified and unsubstantiated "evidence", as was anticipated, the Senate voted 57 to 43 for acquittal, which means that once again we see our magical 57 helping to define a period initiated by the end of the 57th quadrennial cycle on 20 January 2017.

History will note that Trump became the only President to be impeached and acquitted twice – first for adhering to his Presidential and Constitutional duty by requesting investigatory information as dictated by the 1998 US-Ukraine treaty.

As pervasive as the presented Swamp Denizen lie was, the fact remains that the motivation for the invocation of the treaty was the former Vice President, now newly elected President, appearing in an international forum and publically boasting of how he engaged in a *quid pro quo* blackmail resulting in the firing the Ukraine Prosecutor General and his subsequently with an engineer and convicted felon who had just been released from jail. In order to meet the blackmail demand, it required an act of Ukraine's Parliament to create a special qualification exemption.

Then we have the second impeachment involving political rhetoric that was labeled insurrection after protesting election results that, while consistent with a POTUS Cousin 4-Sisters pattern, defied the historical election pattern in which a sitting President who gains votes during his run for reelection is the winner of that secoond election. And once more, accusing the President produced what can only be termed a no-investigation no-witnesses required indictment in a kangaroo-court that then saw a trial that openly and explicitly violated a primary article of the Constitution [#A1S3C6], that would be ignored in favor of the more easily comprehended reality focuesed upon by Senate Minority Leader Mitch McConnell .

Senator McConnell declared the process unconstitutional: "*I believe the best constitutional reading shows that Article II, Section 4 exhausts the set of persons who can legitimately be impeached, tried or convicted.   It's the president, the vice president and civil officers. We have no power to convict and disqualify a former officeholder who is now a private citizen."*

Basically, McConnell correctly stated the matter became moot as soon as Biden was inaugurated as the result of a lawful election.

The purpose of impeachment is removal, not prosecution – or, we could state the purpose is removal to allow criminal prosecution. If a President resigns before the natural expiration of their term, they remain subject to impeachment – but, legally and rationally, the vote on impeachment must occur before they exit office. This was done, post election, with Trump, whose lawful exit was noon on 20 January 2021.

The Swamp Denizens have made it clear they will continue to distract the public by pursuing criminal cases against Trump, even though they once again failed to cite a even a single criminal statute in their Articles of Impeachment.

Since the first call to impeach, which came on the day after the 2016 election, the world has watched four years of petty vindictive actions by those most threatened by rational policies which place America before the interests of foreign and domestic elite oligarchs who routinely bribe the Denizens.

Accordingly, the Swamp Denizens continue to strive to invent any excuse possible to avoid working in the service or to the benefit of American Citizens. As a P.T. Barnum type, Trump was skilled in taking full advantage of the bias the Swamp has against providing any real national service.

As Trump declared after the acquittal: *"MAGA 'has only just begun' ... Our historic, patriotic and beautiful movement to Make America Great Again has only just begun. In the months ahead, I have much to share with you, and I look forward to continuing our incredible journey together to achieve American greatness for all of our people. ... It is a sad commentary on our times that one political party in America is given a free pass to denigrate the rule of law, defame law enforcement, cheer mobs, excuse rioters, and transform justice into a tool of political vengeance, and persecute, blacklist, cancel and suppress all people and viewpoints with whom or which they disagree. ... I always have, and always will, be a champion for the unwavering rule of law, the heroes of law enforcement, and the right of Americans to peacefully and honorably debate the issues of the day without malice and without hate."*

MSM will be given things to debate while harm is done to the nation by Congressional Swamp Denizens. MSM will also continue to look to Trump for unusual and apolitical responses to the stupidity that has normally controlled the masses.

In March 2014 – the Book, *DEATH OVER LIFE, a Prophecy of America's Destruction*, warned you this would happen.

Fortunately, that warning was ignored and history remained on course. Once again you are being warned, and once again you will ignore the reality that is before your eyes. You will insist upon seeing the *Emperor's New Clothes*.

Given the Constitutional breach represented by the failure of the Chief Justice to preside, Republican Swamp Denizens readily identified themselves by joining their Democratic counterparts.

On 12 February, Senator Ted Cruz acknowledge that the next day would see between 53 and 57 vote to convict. The controlling numbers of 56 and 57 would have been consistent with the pattern of this book series. That we received 57 reflects Senator Sue Collins of Maine demonstrating she can no longer be considered a rational, or in any way intelligent, Senator. With her vote, she went on record as knowingly supporting a gross Constitutional Violation [#A1S3C6].

As pointed out in the 2013 book, *President Ted Cruz: The 2016 Election and America's Future*, Cruz has proved himself to be no stranger to attempts to violate the Constitution. However, ever since Trump "put him in his place" Cruz has used skills acquired as a top Harvard Law scholar for the benefit of the nation. And, it was in that context he was able to say: *"This impeachment trial did nothing to bring the domestic terrorists who committed this heinous attack to justice. It merely satisfied Democrats' desire to once again vent their hatred of Donald Trump and their contempt for the tens of millions of Americans who voted for him."*

These Denizens, who we can now count on to vote against the interest of the American people, are:

- Senator Bill Cassidy who declared *"Our Constitution and our country is more important than any one person. I voted to convict President Trump because he is guilty."* Start with a lie, follow with an apparent lie based on the idea of guilty without a crime that would be supported in a court of law.

- Senator Mitt Romney a RINO whose previous record shows his contempt for the nation. He even expressed as justification that which he truly hoped would become the reality. The idea that, somehow, "*President Trump incited the insurrection against Congress by using the power of his office to summon his supporters to Washington on January 6th and urging them to march on the Capitol during the counting of electoral votes. He did this despite the obvious and well known threats of violence that day.*" With that last sentence, it would seem Romney actually defended Trump – made him a dup for those who had actually planned and carried out the mob violence which was condoned by House Democrats when committed by activists against Black communities and State Capitols.

- Senator Ben Sasse who declared: "*An impeachment trial is a public declaration of what a president's oath of office means and what behavior that oath demands of presidents in the future.*" Meaning, an trail that disobeys the Constitution is the model for how he expects Joe Biden and future presidents to regard that document – with actions that "*are violations of a president's oath of office.*"

- Senator Pat Toomey who, after Trump relied on the statistical models to question the election outcome, claimed Trump that "*began with dishonest, systematic attempts to convince supporters that he had won. His lawful, but unsuccessful, legal challenges failed due to lack of evidence.*" And did so after the second impeachment that was devoid of evidence we, as citizens, could clearly state supported the charges against Trump.

- Senator Susan Collins, usually the only rational voice of reason among Republicans, attacked the case put forth by the House Managers by claiming impeachment trial is not about a "*single word uttered*" by Trump on the day of Jan. 6, but is rather about Trump's "*failure to obey the oath he swore on Jan. 20, 2017.*" But she provided no solid evidence of his failure to obey his oath – and voted to accept the trial, absent Chief Justice John Roberts presiding, and therefore conducted in violation of the Constitutional as requirement that he preside. Her actions negated her excuse and put the lie to the assertion: "*My vote in this trial stems from my own oath and duty to defend the Constitution of the United States. The abuse of power and betrayal of his oath by President Trump meet the constitutional standards of high crime and misdemeanors.*"

And for those reasons, I voted to convict Donald J Trump." With her vote, she disgraced herself in the most significant act of the beginning of her last term as a Senator from Maine – it does not matter if she personally holds that Trump created a "*dangerous situation.*" The ones encouraged by Pelosi, etc are far more dangerous than anything Trump said, and violating #A1S3C6 by not having the Chief Justice preside nullifies the lawful objective Constitutional control over impeachment. If we are to look at "dangerous situations," through her vote, Collins explicitly created one that was terminated only by the acquittal.

- Senator Lisa Murkowski showed wisdom enough to avoid any statement immediately after the vote. But once again, her vote declared she supported the breach of the clear and explicitly stated Constitutional mandate that the Chief Justice preside. Thus she joined ranks with anti-American Swamp Denizens who will ensure *The Most Harm to the Most People* whenever possible.

- Senator Richard Burr voted twice to assert that the trial was unconstitutional, and yet he voted to convict. Why? In his words, even though there was no investigation, no evidence presented to justify the House Impeachment vote, and only pictures of the riot presented to the Senate, he believed there was no question "*The evidence is compelling that President Trump is guilty of inciting an insurrection against a coequal branch of government and that the charge rises to the level of high Crimes and Misdemeanors.*" Yet Burr was still able to state, after having praised the Emperor's New Clothes, "*When this process started, I believed that it was unconstitutional to impeach a president who was no longer in office. I still believe that to be the case.*"

Sorting through the Democrats to distinguish the numerous Swamp Denizens who are in leadership from those petty creatures only seeking to survive is a gargantuan task that will only be achieved over the period in which the nation emerges from the pandemic.

As the Senate moved to vote, MSM had begun to report on what had already been stated earlier in the Trump Card series – the Governor of New York, Andrew Cuomo, might have been complicit with New York City Mayor Bill De Blasio in covering up the number of dead that resulted from packing nursing homes with those caring the Covid-19 virus.

Progressive Democrats and non-swamp dwelling Republicans are joining forces to call for Cuomo's resignation – which means we can expect CNN to turn against the Progressives and undermine the national economic and physical health.

As part of the Cuomo misrepresentation we knew existed and so stated in an earlier volume in this series, it has now been learned that New York's nursing home resident death toll was nearly 15,000, that Cuomo and De Blasio had only reported about 8,500, and that the difference was masked by a failure to report those they relocated to hospitals.

This created two issues identified when researchers pinpointed New York as the epicenter or source of most deaths in the nation.

The first being the relocation of Covid-19 patients into nursing homes where they infected both staff and other patients who would otherwise have been protected from exposure to the culling virus; the second being the echoing of calls like that of Pelosi in San Francisco's Chinatown, which invited people to engage in superspreader activities like using the normally crowded New York City subway system.

As a result of Cuomo's falsehood and mismanagement of the Covid-19 issue, 14 New York State Democratic Senators joined with Republicans in calling for a revocation of Governor Andrew Cuomo's emergency powers. They declared, "*While the executive's authority to issue directives is due to expire on April 30, we urge the Senate to advance and adopt a repeal as expeditiously as possible.*"

Along with the call to strip Cuomo of his emergency powers, on 12 February, State Representative Lee Zeldin tweeted, "*Today, along with the rest of the NY GOP House Delegation, I called on the DOJ to investigate Gov Cuomo and his admin for Obstruction of Justice following a coverup of deaths in NY nursing homes. I joined @AmericaRpts to discuss the demand for accountability.*"

Unlike the attacks on Trump, the crime committed by Cuomo has real victims and identifiable witnesses to his willful participation in both the manipulating and reporting of the falsehood.

The New York Post Editorial Board took matters a step further to call for a Federal investigation of Cuomo's criminal coverup of the deaths. Harkening back to the OJ Simpson example, the placing of infected patients among the target population of the culling virus is in some ways an act of manslaughter or murder and certainly wrongful death for which both Cuomo and De Blasio should be held personally and legally responsible.

Congressman Richard Hudson (R-N.C.) Is on record saying, *"You're either going to stand with the victims in these nursing homes and their families and stand up against politicians who lied and deceived to cover their own tracks, or you're not. ... The only way you're going to get the attention of bureaucrats and politicians like Governor Cuomo is to threaten their funding. And the only way the funding gets cut is if they don't share their data"*

At the same time, 30 members of the Energy and Commerce Committee voted to block an action by Representative and Minority Whip Steve Scalise (R-La.) that would penalize states that undercut and under-reported Covid-19 nursing home deaths.

Thus with the NYS coverup we are seeing an expanded pattern of behavior by the Swamp Denizens to inflict *"The Most Harm on the Most People."* Since we are two years away from the next election, it will be interesting to see how the public reacts to those engineering needless deaths and disruption. With Trump out of office, it will be difficult for the Swamp to deflect blame on him, and they certainly are going to find it awkward to place blame on the new occupant of the Oval Office.

CHAPTER TWELVE – Just Imagine

"Imagine the people who believe such things and who are not ashamed to ignore, totally, all the patient findings of thinking minds through all the centuries since the Bible was written. … it is these ignorant people, the most uneducated, the most unimaginative, the most unthinking among us, who would make themselves the guides and leaders of us all; who would force their feeble and childish beliefs on us;"

~ Isaac Asimov, The Roving Mind

Well, since Trump is out and Biden in, apart from presenting the transcript of his 6 January Speech as the next and final chapter, The Trump Card Series can officially be brought to an end.

So let's have some fun. Let's take a look at the true instigators of national distrust, dissent, disorder, and unrest – MSM Editorial Boards and the incitement which they rely upon to gain readership.

We know the game – Publisher William Randolph Hearst was a person who became famous for it when Hearst Publicans incited the Second Cuban War of Independence and then Spanish American War while in competition with Joseph Pulitzer for New York readers. As a result, the events which began in 1895 carried through as ripples in time to give the United States control over the Philippines and later create the Cuban Revolution that brought Fidel Castro's family into power.

Just imagine, if you can, that there was a time traveler visiting this era to gain first hand knowledge of the details. And, since she or he would have the knowledge held by historians of the future, and knew what they were focusing on, how would he or she report back their findings?

Keep in mind, this is not a Seagate adventure, there is no two way street, when they come back they come to a time they are stuck there and must endeavor to both fit in and not change the events that brought them into existence in their time.

It is, however, somewhat akin to time travel in the Terminator Universe – nothing existing physically outside their body can make the journey with them. And the ripple effect prevents communication using electromagnetic frequencies – be it any frequency range, such as radio, sound, light, or atomic radiation – because they scatter and would influence far beyond the immediate point of use.

Knowing this, it seems perverse to realize the only way time travel could be achieved was to transmit the consciousness of the individual into a body that was both receptive and might otherwise have died or gone unnoticed. The least disruptive emergence being to occupy a fetus, newborn, or possibly a toddler who was involved in some physical accident that should have killed them, but which they "miraculously survive."

If you seek to send a message, use archaeology and prevailing mythology – include a spacesuit on in an ancient carved decoration.

Now that we know the communication problem, how would they report upon the way the Boston Globe Editorial Board described the first impeachment, when every historian of their time knew it was simply based on a misrepresentation of the lawful invocation or use of the Clinton-era Ukraine treaty allowing for the sharing of any and all investigatory findings by one nation that might be relevant to the enforcement of the National Laws or Constitution of the other?

Should our time-visitor laugh or simply shake their head when the violation of the Constitution is described in terms of being "*in the face of a meticulous case brought by nine House prosecutors, they found safe harbor in technical arguments that the trial itself was not valid because Trump was no longer in office.*"

In context, The Globe editors pointed out, this was "*the fourth presidential impeachment trial in U.S. history, and the only one in which the accused had left office before being tried.*"

But our time-visitor would also knew the post-impeachment, post Biden Administration Trump family history. They also had full knowledge of the after effects of the culling pandemic – with all its dozens of mutations – and the economic turmoil that would befall the European Union because of both its handling of BREXIT and the pandemic.

Thus, our visitor reads these things with the both benefit of hindsight and knowledge that they must – much like the way Willy Wonka warned the obstinate girl – issue their warning in a manner that would not change history, but would still be a matter of record.

They had the benefit of hindsight but their own survival and that of their generation depended on their endeavoring not to change events, but rather to place their observations in an archival reference known to survive into the future, where they would be discovered at a point in time after our time-visitor had departed for the past.

Knowing that there had been a revolutionary plot in the works, and that, within a decade, it would devastate several major cities, how would the time traveler report back, or even accept, the reaction to McConnell saying: *"The leader of the free world cannot spend weeks thundering that shadowy forces are stealing our country and then feign surprise when people believe him and do reckless things."*

With the Senate divided equally between the parties, and since Democratic Vice President Kamala Harris has the deciding vote when there was a tie, the Democrats became the majority. Yet the Boston Globe would refer to Senator Chuck Schumer as the "minority leader" in a Senate he effectively controlled, and whose actions were now his responsibility.

Referencing his as the minority leader, the Globe cited him as saying: *"moments after the vote. 'Just look at what has happened. Look at what Republicans have been forced to defend. Look at what Republicans have chosen to forgive.'"*

"Forgive?" What did they forgive? That the House Managers provided the pictures and he provided the war? Were they showing forgiveness when they went along with clear Constitutional violations – most notably the explicit language and mandate of #A1S3C6 that was included in the Defense brief, but ignored when, as the Globe saw no reason to flag it's own statement, Senator Schumer appointed as *"the presiding officer, Sen. Patrick Leahy of Vermont"*?

We know that Chief Justice John Roberts declined the posyt he was mandated by the Constitution to occupy – and yet MSM did not raise any issue with or question about a Chief Justice of the Supreme Court declining a mandated duty associated with his job.

Google "Roberts declined to preside" and we are told *"Roberts refusal to preside means that he believes he is not required to preside. He's also not required to administer the oath of office to the president. Yet it has done it four times."*

And, with the quote, we have a link to a blog by University of Wisconsin Law School Professor Ann Althouse in which she states: *"I can't tell, reading this article, if he was asked to preside and communicated a refusal, or if Senate Democrats decided that the Constitution, Article I, Section 3, does not provide for a role for the Chief Justice."*

HUM. On of the problems of history, many critical things do

not survive through time. And when computer electronic databases are damaged by nuclear EMF waves, many things are lost. Too bad there wasn't a book published during the period in which the events occurred that cited data which would later be lost.

True, nobody would read the book, The surviving copy would later be found among other items belonging to the author.

As with Althouse, on 27 January 2021, the New York Post ran a piece in which it also raised the issue of why Roberts declined what was a clear Constitutional obligation of his role as Chief Justice.

The lede comment in NY Post article was, *"Chief Justice John Roberts' refusal to preside over former President Donald Trump's second impeachment trial is raising questions about whether he views the first-of-its-kind proceedings as constitutional."*

As reported, in an interview on MSNBC's "The Rachel Maddow Show," Schumer offered the excuse, *"The Constitution says the chief justice presides for a sitting president. So it was up to John Roberts whether he wanted to preside with a president who is no longer sitting, Trump, and he doesn't want to do it."*

Thus we have an admission of the unconstitutional nature of the proceedings. The Constitution only allows the impeachment of a sitting president – which Trump was when the House voted – the trial, while mandated in response to the House Articles, became moot and illegal after the inauguration resulting from a lawful removal of that President. Had Trump resigned and had Pence taken over – as Pelosi wanted – matters [legal facts] would have been different.

As established with the impeachment trial of Secretary of War William Belknap in 1876, you cannot resign to avoid a prosecution for your actions. As we know, Nixon resigned prior to impeachment and then Ford gave him protective cover by issuing a pardon,

As Senator Rand Paul (R-Ky.) wrote in an op-ed for The Hill, *"The Constitution says two things about impeachment — it is a tool to remove the officeholder, and it must be presided over by the Chief Justice of the Supreme Court."*

Thus, given what was available prior to the Trial – via a simple Google search – there was a well defined lack of any Constitutional basis for the Senate Trial, the #A1S3C6 requirement that the Chief Justice preside does not apply to an illegal act committed by the various members of Congress [House and Senate] in violation of the members Oath of Office, and promoting that illegality constitutes an open attack on the foundation of the American Legal system.

Of course, as stated by Isaac Asimov, the mystical 57 became the number of individuals who understood exactly how ignorant the average American is – and immediately, that average American was willing to proclaim and affirm their ignorance.

Are our elected representative truly *"the most uneducated, the most unimaginative, the most unthinking among us"*?

Or, is it the voter who placed them in that position of trust and honor?

The Constitution talks about the *"sole Power"* of the Senate *"to try all Impeachments"* and mandates that *"When the President of the United States is tried the Chief Justice shall preside; And no Person shall be convicted without the Concurrence of two thirds of the Members present."* Thus a rational voter would first ask if Donald John Trump was the *"President of the United States"* being tried?

According to the Constitution, and the Inauguration held on 20 January 2021, Joseph R Biden was and is *"President of the United States."* Donald John Trump does not hold any political office – the position he now holds is one of honor. He is the FORMER *"President of the United States;"* the 44th person to hold that office and the head of the 45th Administration which came into being the end of the 57th quadrennial cycle on 20 January 2017 and is historically designated as defining the 58th quadrennial cycle.

President Biden played to the idiots by stating, with regard to the Trump acquittal: '*Substance of the charge is not in dispute.*'

But the reality is that a "charge" does not mean there is cause or substance. If it did, then every man and woman who was charged with witchcraft in the 1600s was charged with something that was or is a scientifically and objectively provable real thing.

Even asserting that the '*Substance of the [witchcraft] charge is not in dispute,*' it would not establish guilt. However, this is 2021, and charging someone with witchcraft – speaking words that traveled back in time so people could arm themselves and acquire body armor – obvious is to charge them with something that is real.

The magical spell is fantastic. Speak the words and invoke the spell today and the magic travels backward through time so that all the elements of violence and self-protection can be prepared to use – and then are used even before, or concurrent with, the words being spoken.

The Charge of insurrection based on a speech that, as AOC and the rest of the pro-Clinton Democrats did in 2016, questioned the validity of the Electoral College.

Biden has no problem letting it be know he considers average voters to be as dumb as those in Salem February 1692 and May 1693. And why is there the coincidence – the current Witchcraft assertion is happening at the same time of year as the one 329 years earlier?

Are American voters suffer from some form of mass hysteria?

As an historic first they have twice tolerated the disruption of Impeachment without either evidence or primary witness testimony. We have supposedly ration representative bemoaning the fact that a former president was not found guilty in an action intended for a sitting president where the only evidentiary testimony is a third party claim to hearsay information.

Worse, the objective facts, as presented in the Constitutional mandate, show that it was, by a vote to 232 to 197, that the House of Representatives revealed its devotion to violating the Constitution and rule of law by, for the second time, voting impeachment without firsthand evidence or even legal cause. Unless voters choose to hold that obedience to a valid treaty – entered into by President William Clinton – is a lawful cause of action. If so, henceforth, no President shall honor any treaty entered into by a predecessor – or they will be impeached for that High Crime.

If we follow the TDS suffering Editorial Boards, we see that they are playing to the fools, ignorant, and uneducated.

As with Warren's Boston, Schumer's New York produced an editorial board opinion of Trump guilt. As obvious as it seemed to these MSM types, when the prosecutors asked for witnesses all they could produce was an affidavit of one individual's unsupported hearsay that was not even relevant to the charge of insurrection.

In response, the Defense stated it would produce witnesses. Immediately, rather than risk having their fraud proven, the prosecution dropped the idea of having any witnesses.

The NYTIMES declared that, *"To excuse Mr. Trump's attack on American democracy would invite more such attempts, by him and by other aspiring autocrats. The stakes could not be higher."*

Yet, as the facts reveal, it was the prosecutors who violated the Constitution's #A1S3C6 mandate to have John Roberts preside; it was the prosecution that went out of its way to attack as many

Constitutional articles as they could; it was the prosecution who invoked emotional responses rather than present hard evidence.

The Times board fell back on a practice followed since the 2016 results were announced, as with the quid pro quo blackmail, they accuse Trump of doing what their side was proven to have done and had even boasted of doing. In that regard, they wrote, "*Once again, Mr. Trump has played his most devoted supporters for suckers and insulted the intelligence of the rest of the American people.*"

What of Warren's Boston?

Residents of Boston can take great pride in the Globe returning them to their puritanical accused witch-burning tradition – a time or mentality two centuries before the Constitution and due process that accompanies the rule of law rather than superstitious bigotry and the blatant disregard for reality typified by the founders of boston.

The day before the Senators voted, the Boston Globe Editorial Board declared, "*Do your job, Senate*"

In keeping with the title of this volume, we can say that, on 12 February 2021, the editorial board of the Boston Globe showed its desire to serve Satan with the words "*Do your job, Senate.*" But they did not want the Senate to do its job, they were, in truth, beseeching it to violate the Constitution and undermine the very foundation of American reason and justice.

To the Globe, legality, Constitutionality, and consistency with procedural policies, should be abandoned in favor of vengeance over the failure of those acting dishonestly to hold a dishonest trial, in the absence of the lawfully designated legal overseer, after four years of seeking some basis to impeach a lawfully elected president.

Remember the 2021 impeachment proceedings resulted from an objective first asserted the day after the 2016 election – the first draft articles of impeachment having been submitted to the House a month before the 2017 Inauguration ... a month before Trump took office.

After numerous failures to find a valid charge upon which to hang their indictment, the House settled on the lawful response to Joe Biden bragging that, as Vice President, with the full consent and approval of President Barack Obama, he successfully committed the *quid pro quo bribery* of the Ukraine government. Subsequently, it was learned that this was apparently done for personal financial gain and protection of Hunter Biden, the Vice President's son.

But even while the indictment succeeded, the Senate could not bring itself to convict a President for invoking a lawful treaty that was designed to obtain details of the specific involvement of American citizens in crimes committed in, or being investigated by, Ukraine government entities.

Worse, the Impeachment was brought in the face of a freely given *prima facie* confession to the deed – utilizing a treat of blocking or withholding federal funds unless a high government official were terminate and replaced by someone lacking the basic requirement for the vacated position.

The Globe's Editorial Board looked at the Senate, and asserted it was "*their cowardice at that impeachment trial*" that created the drama in which "*those senators nearly paid with their lives,*" and the reason that "*Days later, two more police officers died by suicide.*"

Police committed suicide because a dishonest impeachment failed?

Both District of Columbia Officer Jeffrey Smith, and Capitol Police Officer Howard Liebengood apparently "*took their own lives in the aftermath of that battle,*" and a third Officer, Brian Sicknick, "*died from injuries he sustained during the Capitol attack.*"

In addition, five other people died in the attack. Did Congress investigate to discover the true cause of the events? Did Congress seek to discover what other stressors might have contributed to the suicides? Did they even care? The evidence shows they immediately engaged in an illegal impeachment that duplicated the first illegal one.

We now know that intelligence agencies had "*ample evidence an angry mob would descend on Washington,*" that they provided prior knowledge – which should have been available to the Speaker of the House – and yet the security personnel failed to "*act on this intelligence or adequately prepare for the looming threat.*" At least that seemed to be the viewpoint of House Appropriations Chair Rosa DeLauro (D-Conn.).

According to media reports, the problems emerging on 6 January were know to exist and be in the planning stage days and/or weeks before the event. But there is no indication that anyone in the Trump administration was involved in the planning. We also know of the long history of Pelosi and others among the accusers calling for people to violently take to the streets – even their openly condoning attacks in Portland. So there is ample evidence of the propaganda that made the violence acceptable being generated by those who accused Trump. And remember, they also accused Trump of the *quid pro quo* action Biden boasted about.

The Globe editors later asserted that a failure to convict a second time – after the President had be lawfully voted out of office and his successor inaugurated – "*would turn the Senate's power to disqualify into a nullity, allowing any president or federal official facing conviction in the future to dodge disqualification simply by resigning the moment before the vote.*"

In effect, the editors exposed their lack of coherent logic. They held that, one must always act to achieve that which has already been achieved – even when the action is illegal and would achieve nothing.

They argued a procedural nullification would emerge from a case where the facts were completely unrelated to the law. Legally, if a charge is brought before the lawful term ends, the process continues to fruition – though the judge might lawfully determine the matter at hand to be moot and terminate the proceedings. In effect, that is exactly what Justice Roberts did when he declined to preside.

And this raises a Constitutional issue regarding the judge.

Any lawful trial must be presided over by a lawfully designated justice. In the case of a Presidential impeachment, under Article 1, Section 3, Clause 6 of the Constitution (#A1S3C6), that justice MUST be the Chief Justice of the Supreme Court and not some Senator who is arbitrarily selected based on an Election whose outcome was the subject of contention in the matter underlying the impeachment.

Had the election results been slightly different, the Republican would have retained their control and any presiding Senator would have been a Republican. In which case, the House would not have rushed to have their last minute Kangaroo Court based on the idea of the accused being "Guilty until Proved innocent" under conditions of a Witch Trial where the judgement is based on trial by water – tied the accused to a chair and submerge them, if they drown they are innocent, if they do not, they are clearly magical and guilty.

The Boston Globe, Massachusetts Senator Elizabeth Warren, and all others involve are proudly pushing for a return to the Salem standard of judicial determination.

To the Electoral Board, the matter was now in the hands of "*craven Republicans looking for any excuse to avoid acknowledging*

Trump's guilt" and *"when the trial concludes, they [would] have an opportunity to rectify last year's mistake — or repeat it, and again betray their oath to defend the Constitution against all enemies."*

It is curious that defending the Constitution equates to convicting without evidence. And the purpose of a second trial is to rectify having previously acquitted because a President who honored a valid treaty and his oath of office. It is, clearly, henceforth a High Crime to honor an Oath of Office – hence the clear and compelling evidence of 289 elected members of the Legislative Branch being so proud to have violated their Oath of Office.

It is even more telling that defending the Constitution is an act that involves condoning a political party bringing the charges before a tribunal that is convened in violation of #A1S3C6. At the very least, when Roberts declined, he should have been by MSM to explain the legal basis for his refusal to comply with #A1S3C6.

Defending the Constitution involves denying the defendant a right to counsel, denial of evidence of wrongdoing, denial of any due process, and holding a judicial indictment proceeding that took less time than a Thanksgiving dinner held by puritanical witch-hunters.

If you still don't get it, read the Transcript of Trump's speech and find any place where he incites insurrection. Find any place where he is calling for *"The Storming of the Bastille"* and beheading of the nobility.

You can find support for government attacking actions in the words of Speaker of the House Nancy Pelosi and many members of the House of Representatives.

They attack Republicans.

They have openly and proudly advocated evicting members of the Trump Administration from public places.

If there were grounds for me supporting these members of my Party – the political party I have been a member of for over half a century – it would be great. Donald is an easy target – if you stick to the truth. But they prefer to lie. Lies serve the MSM and give them airtime they are too incompetent to obtain honestly.

But these are fraudulent Democrats – DINOs – Both "In Name Only" and based on their archaic policies, in reality, Dinosaurs. They will soon be extinct. As with the political parasites living off them.

Just imagine…

CHAPTER THIRTEEN – ?Insurrection Speech?
"Donald Trump Speech "Save America"
Rally Transcript January 6"
~ Public Transcript

From the announcement of the election results in November 2016, to the Biden Inauguration, and throughout his first 100 days in office, there has been one goal – Impeach Trump.

Who's goal?

Why that's the Swamp Denizens and all those nations that would prosper if America no longer held a leadership position on the World Stage. America needs to fall – nations that dominate global events generally do so for about 250 years and then either fall by the wayside or are reconstituted into another force that lasts about 250 years.

One of the greatest exceptions has been China, which has never sought world domination in any are but the mercantile. China is, in its classic form, the merchant to the world. It sits to the side and allows other nations to fight to be "Number One" and so is able to survive. The exception being when the Mongolians took over and a fellow named Temüjin led an invasion of China, took over, and became know to the world as Genghis Kahn.

As of 21 January 2021, America is under the guidance of a fellow name Joseph 'Joe' Robinette Biden Jr. – a fellow who might well be a true "Manchurian Candidate." Based on his 2018 boast, we know he is also "Quid Pro Joe" – a fellow who bragged about doing what the Swamp inferred was the motivation behind Trump's act of invoking Clinton's 1998 criminal investigation information sharing Treaty with the Ukraine.

Throughout the Trump administration, the Swamp displayed a consistent pattern of accusing Trump of criminal acts whenever he complied with the laws, treaties, or Constitution.

In January 2021, the House Denizens took only a few hours to push through an historic second impeachment charging Trump with inciting Insurrection based on the speech which appears below.

Read it. Find the words that called for the overthrow of the government. Keep in mind that, on 9 January, a identified as M. Dowling wrote a piece for the NYTimes which stated: "Speaker Pelosi spoke with General Milley, the chairman of the Joint Chiefs of Staff, about making certain President Trump couldn't launch a nuke. She also suggested they remove the President with a military coup."

As you read Trump's speech, keep in mind that a "Military Coup" complies with the definition of "Armed Insurrection" and it was Nancy Pelosi who was calling for it.

Thus we are told that Nancy Pelosi was proactively engaged in an act of sedition that resulted in Dowing writing, "She should be arrested. The woman is dangerous in addition to evil." But, of course, Pelosi and her crew are "Above the Law" and immune from any legal action. It doesn't matter that the witness against her could be General Milley, the chairman of the Joint Chiefs of Staff, as we saw with the second impeachment, there is no need for witnesses or evidence when Pelosi attacks someone, and when the witness exists against her, nobody has the nerve to hold her accountable.

So read, find anything in the speech that even hints at what Pelsoi actually did, and let its existence be known. But also keep in mind that the Impeachment of a private citizen – which Trump is – is unconstitutional and to attempt it is to violate the sworn oath take by all members of Congress.

Here is what was said:

Donald Trump: (02:44)

The media will not show the magnitude of this crowd. Even I, when I turned on today, I looked, and I saw thousands of people here, but you don't see hundreds of thousands of people behind you because they don't want to show that. We have hundreds of thousands of people here, and I just want them to be recognized by the fake news media. Turn your cameras please and show what's really happening out here because these people are not going to take it any longer. They're not going to take it any longer. Go ahead. Turn your cameras, please. Would you show? They came from all over the world, actually, but they came from all over our country. I just really want to see what they do. I just want to see how they covered. I've never seen anything like it. But it would be really great if we could be covered fairly by the media. The media is the biggest problem we have as far as I'm concerned, single biggest problem, the fake news and the big tech. Big tech is now coming into their own. We beat them four years ago. We surprised them. We took them by surprise and this year, they rigged an election. They rigged it like they've never rigged an election before. By the way, last night, they didn't do a bad job either, if you notice. I'm honest. I just, again, I want to thank you. It's just a great honor to have this kind of crowd and to be before you. Hundreds of thousands of American patriots are committed to the honesty of our elections and the integrity of our glorious Republic. All of us here today do not want to see our election victory stolen by emboldened radical left Democrats, which is what they're doing and stolen by the fake news media. That's what they've done and what they're doing. We will never give up. We will never concede, it doesn't happen. You don't concede when there's theft involved.

Donald Trump: (04:42)

Our country has had enough. We will not take it anymore and that's what this is all about. To use a favorite term that all of you people really came up with, we will stop the steal. Today I will lay out just some of the evidence proving that we won this election, and we won it by a landslide. This was not a close election. I say sometimes jokingly, but there's no joke about it, I've been in two elections. I won them both and the second one, I won much bigger than the first. Almost 75 million people voted for our campaign, the most of any incumbent president by far in the history of our country, 12 million more people than four years ago. I was told by the real pollsters, we do have real pollsters. They know that we were going to do well, and we were going to win. What I was told, if I went from 63 million, which we had four years ago to 66 million, there was no chance of losing. Well, we didn't go to 66. We went to 75 million and they say we lost. We didn't lose.

Donald Trump: (06:08)

By the way, does anybody believe that Joe had 80 million votes? Does anybody believe that? He had 80 million computer votes. It's a disgrace. There's never been anything like that. You could take third world countries. Just take a look, take third world countries. Their elections are more honest than what we've been going through in this country. It's a disgrace. It's a disgrace. Even when you look at last night, they're all running around like chickens with their heads cut off with boxes. Nobody knows what the hell is going on. There's never been anything like this. We will not let them silence your voices.

We're not going to let it happen. Not going to let it happen.

Crowd: (07:11)
Fight for Trump! Fight for Trump! Fight for Trump!

Donald Trump: (07:11)
Thank you. I'd love to have, if those tens of thousands of people would be allowed, the military, the secret service, and we want to thank you, and the police law enforcement. Great. You're doing a great job, but I'd love it if they could be allowed to come up here with us. Is that possible? Can you just let them come up, please? Rudy, you did a great job. He's got guts. You know what? He's got guts, unlike a lot of people in the Republican party. He's got guts, he fights. He fights, and I'll tell you. Thank you very much, John. Fantastic job. I watched. That's a tough act to follow, those two. John is one of the most brilliant lawyers in the country, and he looked at this and he said, "What an absolute disgrace, that this could be happening to our constitution." He looked at Mike Pence, and I hope Mike is going to do the right thing.

Donald Trump: (08:09)
I hope so. I hope so because if Mike Pence does the right thing, we win the election. All he has to do. This is from the number one or certainly one of the top constitutional lawyers in our country. He has the absolute right to do it. We're supposed to protect our country, support our country, support our constitution, and protect our constitution. States want to revote. The States got defrauded. They were given false information. They voted on it. Now they want to recertify. They want it back. All Vice-President Pence has to do is send it back to the States to recertify, and we become president, and you are the happiest people.

Donald Trump: (09:08)
I just spoke to Mike. I said, "Mike, that doesn't take courage. What takes courage is to do nothing. That takes courage," and then we're stuck with a president who lost the election by a lot, and we have to live with that for four more years. We're just not going to let that happen. Many of you have traveled from all across the nation to be

here, and I want to thank you for the extraordinary love. That's what it is. There's never been a movement like this ever, ever for the extraordinary love for this amazing country and this amazing movement. Thank you.

Crowd: (09:44)
We love Trump! We love Trump! We love Trump!

Donald Trump: (09:59)
By the way, this goes all the way back past the Washington monument. Do you believe this? Look at this. Unfortunately, they gave the press the prime seats. I can't stand that. No, but you look at that behind. I wish they'd flip those cameras and look behind you. That is the most amazing sight. When they make a mistake, you get to see it on television. Amazing, amazing, all the way back. Don't worry. We will not take the name off the Washington monument. We will not. Cancel culture. They wanted to get rid of the Jefferson Memorial, either take it down or just put somebody else in there. I don't think that's going to happen. It damn well better not. Although with this administration, if this happens, it could happen. You'll see some really bad things happen.

Donald Trump: (10:54)
They'll knock out Lincoln too, by the way. They've been taking his statue down, but then we signed a little law. You hurt our monuments, you hurt our heroes, you go to jail for 10 years and everything stopped. Did you notice that? It stopped. It all stopped. They could use Rudy back in New York City. Rudy, they could use you. Your city is going to hell. They want Rudy Giuliani back in New York. We'll get a little younger version of Rudy. Is that okay, Rudy?

Donald Trump: (11:25)
We're gathered together in the heart of our nation's Capitol for one very, very basic and simple reason, to save our democracy. Most candidates on election evening, and of course this thing goes on so long, they still don't have any idea what the votes are. We still have congressional seats under review. They have no idea. They've totally lost control. They've used the pandemic as a way of defrauding the

people in a proper election. But when you see this and when you see what's happening, number one, they all say, "Sir, we'll never let it happen again." I said, "That's good, but what about eight weeks ago?" They try and get you to go. They say, "Sir, in four years, you're guaranteed." I said, "I'm not interested right now. Do me a favor, go back eight weeks. I want to go back eight weeks. Let's go back eight week." We want to go back, and we want to get this right because we're going to have somebody in there that should not be in there and our country will be destroyed, and we're not going to stand for that.

Donald Trump: (12:34)

For years, Democrats have gotten away with election fraud and weak Republicans, and that's what they are. There's so many weak Republicans. We have great ones, Jim Jordan, and some of these guys. They're out there fighting the House. Guys are fighting, but it's incredible. Many of the Republicans, I helped them get in. I helped them get elected. I helped Mitch get elected. I could name 24 of them, let's say. I won't bore you with it, and then all of a sudden you have something like this. It's like, "Gee, maybe I'll talk to the president sometime later." No, it's amazing. The weak Republicans, they're pathetic Republicans and that's what happens. If this happened to the Democrats, there'd be hell all over the country going on. There'd be hell all over the country. But just remember this. You're stronger, you're smarter. You've got more going than anybody, and they try and demean everybody having to do with us, and you're the real people. You're the people that built this nation. You're not the people that tore down our nation.

Donald Trump: (13:45)

The weak Republicans, and that's it. I really believe it. I think I'm going to use the term, the weak Republicans. You got a lot of them, and you got a lot of great ones, but you got a lot of weak ones. They've turned a blind eye even as Democrats enacted policies that chipped away our jobs, weakened our military, threw open our borders and put America last. Did you see the other day where Joe Biden said, "I want to get rid of the America first policy." What's that all about, get rid of ...? How do you say, "I want to get rid of America first?" Even if you're going to do it, don't talk about it. Unbelievable, what we have to go through, what we have to go through and you have to get your people to fight. If they don't fight, we have to primary the hell out of the ones that don't fight. You primary them. We're going to let you know who they are. I can already tell you, frankly.

Donald Trump: (14:39)

But this year using the pretext of the China virus and the scam of mail-in ballots, Democrats attempted the most brazen and outrageous election theft. There's never been anything like this. It's a pure theft in American history, everybody knows it. That election, our election was over at 10:00 in the evening. We're leading Pennsylvania, Michigan, Georgia by hundreds of thousands of votes, and then late in the evening or early in the morning, boom, these explosions of and bullshit, and all of a sudden. All of a sudden it started to happen.

Crowd: (15:25)

[inaudible 00:15:25]

Donald Trump: (15:35)

Don't forget when Romney got beat. Romney. I wonder if he enjoyed his flight in last night? But when Romney got beaten, he stands up like you're more typical. Well, I'd like to congratulate the victor, the victor. Who was the victor, Mitt? I'd like to congratulate. They don't go and look at the facts. Now I don't know. He got slaughtered probably, maybe it was okay. Maybe it was that's what happened. But we look at the facts and our lecture was so corrupt that in the history of this country, we've never seen anything like it. You can go all the way back. America is blessed with elections all over the world. They talk about our elections. You know what the world says about us now? They said we don't have free and fair elections and you know what else? We don't have a free and fair press.

Donald Trump: (16:25)

Our media is not free. It's not fair. It suppresses thought. It suppresses speech, and it's become the enemy of the people. It's become the enemy of the people. It's the biggest problem we have in this country. No third world countries would even attempt to do what we caught them doing and you'll hear about that in just a few minutes. Republicans are constantly fighting like a boxer with his hands tied behind his back. It's like a boxer, and we want to be so nice. We want to be so respectful of everybody, including bad people. We're going to have to fight much harder and Mike Pence is going to have to come through for us. If he doesn't, that will be a sad day for our country because you're sworn to uphold our constitution. Now it is up to Congress to confront this egregious assault on our democracy. After this, we're going to walk down and I'll be there with you. We're going to walk down. We're going to walk down any one you want, but I think right here. We're going walk down to the Capitol, and we're going to cheer on our brave senators, and congressmen and women. We're probably not going to be cheering so much for some of them because you'll never take back our country with weakness. You have to show strength, and you have to be strong.

Donald Trump: (18:16)

We have come to demand that Congress do the right thing and only count the electors who have been lawfully slated, lawfully slated. **I know that everyone here will soon be marching over to the Capitol building to peacefully and patriotically make your voices heard.** Today we will see whether Republicans stand strong for integrity of our elections, but whether or not they stand strong for our country, our country. Our country has been under siege for a long time, far longer than this four-year period. We've set it on a much straighter course, a much … I thought four more years. I thought it would be easy. We created-

Donald Trump: (19:03)

Four more years, I thought it would be easy. We created the greatest economy in history. We rebuilt our military. We get you the biggest tax cuts in history. We got you the biggest regulation cuts. There's no President, whether it's four years, eight years, or in one case more, got anywhere near the regulation cuts. It used to take 20 years to get a highway approved. now we're down to two. I want to get it down to one, but we're down to two. And it may get rejected for environmental or safety reasons, but we got it down the safety. We created Space Force. Look at what we did. Our military has been totally rebuilt. So we create Space Force, which by in of itself is a major achievement for an administration. And with us, it's one of so many different things.

Donald Trump: (19:52)

Right to try. Everybody know about right to try. We did things that nobody ever thought possible. We took care of our vets. Our vets, the VA now has the highest rating, 91%, the highest rating that it's had from the beginning, 91% approval rating. Always you watch the VA, when it was on television. Every night people living in a horrible, horrible manner. We got that done. We got accountability done. We got it so that now in the VA, you don't have to wait for four weeks, six weeks, eight weeks, four months to see a doctor. If you can't get a doctor, you go outside you get the doctor, you have them taken care of. And we pay the doctor. And we've not only made life wonderful for so many people, we've saved tremendous amounts of money, far secondarily, but we've saved a lot of money.

Donald Trump: (20:49)

And now we have the right to fire bad people in the VA. We had 9000 people that treated our veterans horribly. In primetime, they would not have treated our veterans badly. But they treated our veterans horribly. And we have what's called the VA Accountability Act. And the accountability says if we see somebody in there that doesn't treat our vets well, or they steal, they rob, they do things badly. We say, "Joe, you're fired. Get out of here." Before you couldn't do that. You couldn't do that before.

Donald Trump: (21:24)

So we've taken care of things. We've done things like nobody's ever thought possible. And that's part of the reason that many people don't like us, because we've done too much, but we've done it quickly. And we were going to sit home and watch a big victory. And everybody had us down for a victory. It was going to be great. And now we're out here fighting. I said to somebody, I was going to take a few days and relax after our big electoral victory. Ten o'clock, it was over. But I was going to take a few days.

Donald Trump: (21:52)

And I can say this, since our election, I believe, which was a catastrophe when I watch and even these guys knew what happened, they know what happened. They're saying, "Wow, Pennsylvania's insurmountable. Wow, Wisconsin, look at the big leads we had." Even though the press said we were going to lose Wisconsin by 17 points. Even though the press said Ohio is going to be close, we set a record. Florida's going to be close, we set a record. Texas is going to be close. Texas is going to be close, we set a record. And we set a record with Hispanic, with the Black community. We set a record with everybody.

Donald Trump: (22:36)

Today, we see a very important event though, because right over there, right there, we see the event going to take place. And I'm going to be watching, because history is going to be made. We're going to see whether or not we have great and courageous leaders or whether or not we have leaders that should be ashamed of themselves throughout history, throughout eternity, they'll be ashamed. And you know what? If they do the wrong thing, we should never ever forget that they did. Never forget. We should never ever forget. With only three of the seven states in question, we win the presidency of the United States.

Donald Trump: (23:21)

And by the way, it's much more important today than it was 24 hours ago. Because I spoke to David Perdue, what a great person, and Kelly Loeffler, two great people, but it was a setup. And I said, "We have no back line anymore." The only back line, the only line of demarcation, the only line that we have is the veto of the president of the United States. So this is now what we're doing, a far more important election than it was two days ago.

Donald Trump: (23:59)

I want to thank the more than 140 members of the House. Those are warriors. They're over there working like you've never seen before, studying, talking, actually going all the way back, studying the roots of the Constitution, because they know we have the right to send a bad vote that was illegally got, they gave these people bad things to vote for and they voted, because what did they know? And then when they found out a few weeks later... Again, it took them four years to devise history. And the only unhappy person in the United States, single most unhappy, is Hillary Clinton because she said, "Why didn't you do this for me four years ago? Why didn't you do this for me four years ago? Change the votes! 10,000 in Michigan. You could have changed the whole thing!" But she's not too happy. You notice you don't see her anymore. What happened? Where is Hillary? Where is she?

Donald Trump: (24:57)

But I want to thank all of those congressmen and women. I also want to thank our 13 most courageous members of the US Senate, Senator Ted Cruz, Senator Ron Johnson, Senator Shadowless, Kelly Loeffler. And Kelly Loeffler, I'll tell you, she's been so great. She works so hard. So let's give her and David a little special head, because it was rigged against them. Let's give her and David. Kelly Loeffler, David Perdue. They fought a good race. They never had a shot. That equipment should never have been allowed to be used, and I was telling these people don't let them use this stuff. Marsha Blackburn, terrific person. Mike Braun, Indiana. Disinvested, great guy. Bill Hagerty, John Kennedy, James Lankford, Cynthia Lummis. Tommy Tuberville, to the coach. And Roger Marshall. We want to thank them, senators that stepped up, we want to thank them.

Donald Trump: (26:04)

I actually think though it takes, again, more courage not to step up. And I think a lot of those people are going to find that out, and you better start looking at your leadership because the leadership has led you down the tubes. "We don't want to give $2000 to people. We want to give them $600." Oh, great. How does that play politically? Pretty good? And this has nothing to do with politics. But how does it play politically? China destroyed these people. We didn't destroy. China destroyed them, totally destroyed them. We want to give them $600, and they just wouldn't change. I said, "Give them $2000. We'll pay it back. We'll pay it back fast. You already owe 26 trillion. Give them a couple of bucks. Let them live. Give them a couple of bucks!"

Donald Trump: (26:57)

And some of the people here disagree with me on that. But I just say, look, you got to let people live. And how does that play though? Okay, number one, it's the right thing to do. But how does that play politically? I think it's the primary reason, one of the primary reasons, the other was just pure cheating. That was the super primary reason.

But you can't do that. You got to use your head.

Donald Trump: (27:19)

As you know the media is constantly asserted the outrageous lie that there was no evidence of widespread fraud. You ever see these people? "While there is no evidence of fraud…" Oh, really? Well, I'm going to read you pages. I hope you don't get bored listening to it. Promise? Don't get bored listening to it, all those hundreds of thousands of people back there. Move them up, please. Yeah. All these people don't get bored. Don't get angry at me because you're going to get bored because it's so much. The American people do not believe the corrupt fake news anymore. They have ruined their reputation.

Donald Trump: (27:57)

But it used to be that they'd argue with me, I'd fight. So I'd fight, they'd fight. I'd fight, they'd fight. Boop-boop. You'd believe me, you'd believe them. Somebody comes out. They had their point of view, I had my point of view. But you'd have an argument. Now what they do is they go silent. It's called suppression. And that's what happens in a communist country. That's what they do. They suppress. You don't fight with them anymore, unless it's a bad. They have a little bad story about me, they'll make it 10 times worse and it's a major headline. But Hunter Biden, they don't talk about him. What happened to Hunter? Where's Hunter? Where is Hunter? They don't talk about him.

Donald Trump: (28:34)

Now watch all the sets will go off. Well, they can't do that because they get good ratings. The ratings are too good. Now where is Hunter? And how come Joe was allowed to give a billion dollars of money to get rid of the prosecutor in Ukraine? How does that happen? I'd ask you that question. How does that happen? Can you imagine if I said that? If I said that it would be a whole different ball game. And how come Hunter gets three and a half million dollars from the Mayor of Moscow's wife, and gets hundreds of thousands of dollars to sit on an energy board even though he admits he has no knowledge of energy, and millions of dollars up front, and how come they go into China and they leave with billions of dollars to manage?

"Have you managed money before?" "No, I haven't." "Oh, that's good. Here's about 3 billion."

Donald Trump: (29:29)

No, they don't talk about that. No, we have a corrupt media. They've gone silent. They've gone dead. I now realize how good it was if you go back 10 years. I realized how good, even though I didn't necessarily love him, I realized how good it was like a cleansing motion. But we don't have that anymore. We don't have a fair media anymore. It's suppression and you have to be very careful with that. And they've lost all credibility in this country. We will not be intimidated into accepting the hoaxes and the lies that we've been forced to believe over the past several weeks. We've amassed overwhelming evidence about a fake election. This is the presidential election. Last night was a little bit better because of the fact that we had a lot of eyes watching one specific state, but they cheated like hell anyway.

Donald Trump: (30:27)

You have one of the dumbest governors in the United States. And when I endorsed him, I didn't know this guy. At the request of David Perdue. He said, "A friend of mine is running for Governor, what's his name." And you know the rest. He was in fourth place, fifth place. I don't know. He was way... He was doing poorly. I endorsed him. He went like a rocket ship and he won. And then I had to beat Stacey Abrams with this guy, Brian Kemp. I had to beat Stacey Abrams and I had to beat Oprah, used to be a friend of mine. I was on her last show. Her last week she picked the five outstanding people. I don't think she thinks that anymore. Once I ran for president, I didn't notice there were too many calls coming in from Oprah. Believe it or not, she used to like me, but I was one of the five outstanding people.

Donald Trump: (31:17)

And I had a campaign against Michelle Obama and Barack Hussein Obama against Stacey. And I had Brian Kemp, he weighs 130 pounds. He said he played offensive line in football. I'm trying to figure that. I'm still trying to figure that out. He said that the other night, "I was an offensive lineman." I'm saying, "Really? That must've been a really small team." But I look at that and I look at what's happened, and he turned out to be a disaster. This stuff happens.

Donald Trump: (31:50)

Look, I'm not happy with the Supreme Court. They love to rule against me. I picked three people. I fought like hell for them, one in particular I fought. They all said, "Sir, cut him loose. He's killing us." The senators, very loyal senators. They're very loyal people. "Sir, cut him loose. He's killing us, sir. Cut him loose, sir." I must've gotten half of the senators. I said, "No, I can't do that. It's unfair to him. And it's unfair to the family. He didn't do anything wrong. They're made up stories." They were all made up stories. He didn't do anything wrong. "Cut him loose, sir." I said, "No, I won't do that." We got him through. And you know what? They couldn't give a damn. They couldn't give a damn. Let them rule the right way, but it almost seems that they're all going out of their way to hurt all of us, and to hurt our country. To hurt our country.

Donald Trump: (32:40)

I read a story in one of the newspapers recently how I control the three Supreme Court justices. I control them. They're puppets. I read it about Bill Barr, that he's my personal attorney. That he'll do anything for me. And I said, "It really is genius," because what they do is that, and it makes it really impossible for them to ever give you a victory, because all of a sudden Bill Barr changed, if you hadn't noticed. I like Bill Barr, but he changed, because he didn't want to be considered my personal attorney. And the Supreme Court, they rule against me so much. You know why? Because the story is I haven't spoken to any of them, any of them, since virtually they got in. But the story is that they're my puppet. That they're puppets. And now that the only way they can get out of that, because they hate that, it's not good on the social circuit. And the only way they get out is to rule against Trump. So let's rule against Trump, and they do that. So I want to congratulate them.

Donald Trump: (33:41)

But it shows you the media's genius. In fact, probably, if I was the media, I'd do it the same way. I hate to say it. But we got to get them straightened out. Today, for the sake of our democracy, for the sake of our Constitution, and for the sake of our children, we lay out the case for the entire world to hear. You want to hear it?

Crowd: (34:04)

Yes!

Donald Trump: (34:06)

In every single swing state, local officials, state officials, almost all Democrats made illegal and unconstitutional changes to election procedures without the mandated approvals by the state legislatures, that these changes paved the way for fraud on a scale never seen before. And I think we'd go a long way outside of our country when I say that.

Donald Trump: (34:34)

So just in a nutshell, you can't make a change on voting for a federal election unless the state legislature approves it. No judge can do it. Nobody can do it, only a legislature. So as an example in Pennsylvania or whatever, you have a Republican legislature, you have a Democrat mayor, and you have a lot of Democrats all over the place. They go to the legislature, the legislature laughs at them. Says, "We're not going to do that." They say, "Thank you very much." And they go and make the changes themselves. They do it anyway. And that's totally illegal. That's totally illegal. You can't do that.

Donald Trump: (35:13)

In Pennsylvania, the Democrat Secretary of State and the Democrat State Supreme Court justices illegally abolished the signature verification requirements just 11 days prior to the election. So think of what they did. No longer is there signature verification. Oh, that's okay. We want voter ID by the way. But no longer is their signature verification, 11 days before the election! They say, "We don't want it." You know why they don't want it? Because they want to cheat. That's the only reason. Who would even think of that? We don't want to verify a signature? There were over 205,000 more ballots counted in Pennsylvania. Now think of this. You had 205,000 more ballots than you had voters. That means you had 200... Where did they come from? You know where they came from? Somebody's imagination. Whatever they needed. So in Pennsylvania you had 205,000 more votes than you had voters! And it's the number is actually much greater than that now. That was as of a week ago. And this is a mathematical impossibility, unless you want to say it's a total fraud. So Pennsylvania was defrauded.

Donald Trump: (36:35)

Over 8000 ballots in Pennsylvania were cast by people whose names and dates of birth match individuals who died in 2020 and prior to the election. Think of that. Dead people! Lots of dead people, thousands. And some dead people actually requested an application. That bothers me even more. Not only are they voting, they want an application to vote. One of them was 29 years ago died. It's incredible.

Donald Trump: (37:05)

Over 14,000 ballots were cast by out-of-state voters. So these are voters that don't live in the state. And by the way, these numbers are what they call outcome determinative. Meaning these numbers far surpass... I lost by a very little bit. These numbers are massive. Massive. More than 10,000 votes in Pennsylvania were illegally counted, even though they were received after Election Day. In other words, "They were received after Election Day, let's count them anyway!" And what they did in many cases is they did fraud. They took the date and they moved it back, so that it no longer is after Election Day. And more than 60,000 ballots in Pennsylvania were reported received back. They got back before they were ever supposedly mailed out. In other words, you got the ballot back before you mailed it!

Donald Trump: (38:03)

... they were supposedly mailed out, in other words, you got the ballot back before you mailed it, which is also logically and logistically impossible. Think of that one. You got the ballot back. Let's send the ballots. Oh, they've already been sent. But we got the ballot back before they were sent. I don't think that's too good.

Donald Trump: (38:23)

Twenty-five thousand ballots in Pennsylvania were requested by nursing home residents, all in a single giant batch, not legal. Indicating an enormous illegal ballot harvesting operation. You're not allowed to do it. It's against the law. The day before the election, the

State of Pennsylvania reported the number of absentee ballots that had been sent out. Yet this number was suddenly and drastically increased by 400,000 people. It was increased. Nobody knows where it came from by 400,000 ballots. One day after the election, it remains totally unexplained. They said, "Well, we can't figure that." Now that's many, many times what it would take to overthrow the state. Just that one element. 400,000 ballots appeared from nowhere, right after the election.

Donald Trump: (39:16)

By the way, Pennsylvania has now seen all of this. They didn't know because it was so quick. They had a vote, they voted, but now they see all this stuff. It's all come to light. Doesn't happen that fast. And they want to re certify their votes. They want to re certify. But the only way that can happen is if Mike Pence agrees to send it back.

Donald Trump: (39:43)

Mike Pence has to agree to send it back. And many people in Congress want it sent back, and take of what you're doing. Let's say you don't do it. Somebody says, "Well, we have to obey the constitution." And you are, because you're protecting our country and you're protecting the constitution, so you are. But think of what happens. Let's say they're stiffs and they're stupid people. And they say, "Well, we really have no choice." Even though Pennsylvania and other states want to redo their votes, they want to see the numbers. They already have the numbers. Go very quickly and they want to redo their legislature because many of these votes were taken as I said, because it wasn't approved by their legislature. That in itself is illegal and then you have the scam and that's all of the things that we're talking about. But think of this: if you don't do that, that means you will have a president of the United States for four years, with his wonderful son.

Donald Trump: (40:50)

You will have a president who lost all of these states, or you will have a president to put it another way, who was voted on by a bunch of stupid people who lost all of these things. You will have an illegitimate president, that's what you'll have. And we can't let that happen. These are the facts that you won't hear from the fake news media. It's all part of the suppression effort. They don't want to talk about it. They don't want to talk about it. In fact, when I started talking about that, I guarantee you a lot of the television sets and a lot of those cameras went off and that's how a lot of cameras back there. But a lot of them went off, but these are the things you don't hear about. You don't hear what you just heard. And I'm going to go over a few more states. But you don't hear it by the people who want to deceive you and demoralize you and control you, big tech, media.

Donald Trump: (41:48)

Just like the suppression polls that said, we're going to lose Wisconsin by 17 points, well we won Wisconsin. They don't have it that way because they lose just by a little sliver. But they had me down the day before Washington Post, ABC poll, down 17 points. I called up a real pollster. I said, "What is that?" "Sir, that's called a suppression poll. I think you're going to win Wisconsin, sir." I said, "But why do they make it four or five points?" "Because then people vote. But when you're down 17, they say, 'Hey, I'm not going to waste my time. I love the president, but there's no way.'" Despite that, we won Wisconsin, you'll see. But that's called suppression because a lot of people, when they see that, it's very interesting. This pollster said, "Sir, if you're down three, four or five people vote. When you go down 17, they say, 'Let's save, let's go and have dinner, and let's watch the presidential defeat tonight on television darling.'"

Donald Trump: (42:49)

And just like the radical left tries to blacklist you on social media, every time I put out a tweet, even if it's totally correct, totally correct. I get a flag. I get a flag. And they also don't let you get out. On Twitter, it's very hard to come on to my account. It's very hard to get out a message. They don't let the message get out nearly like they should, but I've had many people say, "I can't get on your Twitter." I don't care about Twitter. Twitter is bad news. They're all bad news. But you know what? If you want to get out of message. And if you want to go through big tech, social media, they are really, if you're a conservative, if you're a Republican, if you have a big voice, I guess they call it shadow ban. Shadow ban. They shadow ban you and it should be illegal. I've been telling these Republicans get rid of Section 230.

Donald Trump: (43:47)

And for some reason, Mitch and the group, they don't want to put it in there. And they don't realize that that's going to be the end of the Republican party as we know it, but it's never going to be the end of us, never. Let them get out. Let the weak ones get out. This is a time for strength. They also want to indoctrinate your children in school by teaching them things that aren't so. They want to indoctrinate your children. It's all part of the comprehensive assault on our democracy and the American people to finally standing up and saying, "No." This crowd is again a testament to it. I did no advertising. I did nothing. You do have some groups that are big supporters. I want to thank that Amy and everybody, we have some incredible supporters, incredible, but we didn't do anything. This just happened.

Donald Trump: (44:39)

Two months ago, we had a massive crowd come down to Washington. I said, "What are they there for." "Sir, they're there for you." We have nothing to do with it. These groups, they're forming all over the United States. And we got to remember, in a year from now, you're going to start working on Congress. And we got to get rid of the weak congresspeople, the ones that aren't any good, the Liz Cheneys of the world, we got to get rid of them. We got to get rid of them. She never wants a soldier brought home. I've brought a lot of our soldiers home. I don't know, some like it. They're in countries that nobody even knows the name. Nobody knows where they are. They're dying. They're great, but they're dying. They're losing their arms, their legs, their face. I brought them back home, largely back home, Afghanistan, Iraq. Remember I used to say in the old days, "Don't go into Iraq. But if you go in, keep the oil." We didn't keep the oil. So stupid. So stupid, these people. And Iraq has billions and billions of dollars now in the bank. And what did we do? We get nothing. We never get. But we do actually, we kept the oil here. We did good. We got rid of the ISIS caliphate. We got rid of plenty of different things that everybody knows and the rebuilding of our military in three years, people said it couldn't be done. And it was all made in the USA, all made in the USA. Best equipment in the world. In Wisconsin, corrupt Democrat run cities deployed more than 500 illegal unmanned, unsecured drop boxes, which collected a minimum of 91,000 unlawful votes. It was razor thin the loss. This one thing alone is much more than we would need, but there are many things.

Donald Trump: (46:29)

They have these lockboxes and they pick them up and they disappear for two days. People would say, "Where's that box?" They disappeared. Nobody even knew where the hell it was. In addition, over 170,000 absentee votes were counted in Wisconsin without a valid absentee ballot application. So they had a vote, but they had no application. And that's illegal in Wisconsin. Meaning those votes were blatantly done in opposition to state law. And they came 100% from Democrat areas, such as Milwaukee and Madison, 100%. In Madison, 17,000 votes were deposited in so-called human drop boxes. You know what that is, right? Where operatives stuff thousands of unsecured ballots into duffel bags on park benches across the city in complete defiance of cease and desist letters from state legislature. The state legislature said, "Don't do it." They're the only ones that could approve it. They gave tens of thousands of votes.

Donald Trump: (47:37)

They came in in duffel bags. Where the hell did they come from? According to eyewitness testimony, postal service workers in Wisconsin were also instructed to illegally backdate approximately 100,000 ballots. The margin of difference in Wisconsin was less than 20,000 votes. Each one of these things alone wins us the state. Great state, we love the state, we won the state. In Georgia, your secretary of state, I can't believe this guy's a Republican. He loves recording telephone conversations. I thought it was a great conversation personally, so did a lot of other ... people love that conversation, because it says what's going on. These people are crooked. They're 100% in my opinion, one of the most corrupt. Between your governor and your secretary of state. And now you have it again last night, just take a look at what happened, what a mess and the Democrat party operatives entered into an illegal and unconstitutional settlement agreement that drastically weakened signature verification and other election security procedures.

Donald Trump: (48:53)

Stacey Abrams, she took them to lunch and I beat her two years ago with a bad candidate, Brian Kemp. But the Democrats, took the Republicans to lunch because the secretary of state had no clue what the hell was happening, unless he did have a clue. That's interesting.

Maybe he was with the other side, but we've been trying to get verifications of signatures in Fulton County. They won't let us do it. The only reason they won't is because we'll find things in the hundreds of thousands. Why wouldn't they let us verify signatures and Fulton County? Which is known for being very corrupt. They won't do it. They go to some other county where you would live. I said, "That's not the problem. The problem is Fulton County." Home of Stacey Abrams. She did a good job. I congratulate her, but it was done in such a way that we can't let this stuff happen.

Donald Trump: (49:53)

We won't have a country of it happens. As a result Georgia's absentee ballot rejection rate was more than 10 times lower than previous levels, because the criteria was so off, 48 counties in Georgia with thousands and thousands of votes rejected zero ballots. There wasn't one ballot. In other words, in a year in which more mail-in ballots were sent than ever before, and more people were voting by mail for the first time, the rejection rate was drastically lower than it had ever been before. The only way this can be explained is if tens of thousands of illegitimate votes were added to the tally, that's the only way you could explain it. By the way, you're talking about tens of thousands. If Georgia had merely rejected the same number of unlawful ballots, as in other years, there should have been approximately 45,000 ballots rejected, far more than what we needed to win, just over 11,000.

Donald Trump: (50:59)

They should find those votes. They should absolutely find that just over 11,000 votes, that's all we need. They defrauded us out of a win in Georgia, and we're not going to forget it. There's only one reason the Democrats could possibly want to eliminate signature matching, oppose voter ID and stop citizenship confirmation. Are you in citizenship? You're not allowed to ask that question. Because they want to steal the election. The radical left knows exactly what they're doing. They're ruthless and it's time that somebody did something about it. And Mike Pence, I hope you're going to stand up for the good of our constitution and for the good of our country. And if you're not, I'm going to be very disappointed in you. I will tell you right now. I'm not hearing good stories. In Fulton County, republican poll Watchers were rejected in some cases, physically from the room under the false pretense of a pipe burst.

Donald Trump: (52:03)

Water main burst, everybody leave. Which we now know was a total lie. Then election officials pull boxes, Democrats and suitcases of ballots out from under a table. You all saw it on television, totally fraudulent. And illegally scanned them for nearly two hours totally unsupervised. Tens of thousands of votes, as that coincided with a mysterious vote dump of up to 100,000 votes for Joe Biden, almost none for Trump. Oh, that sounds fair. That was at 1:34 AM. The Georgia secretary of state and pathetic governor of Georgia ... although he says, I'm a great president. I sort of maybe have to change. He said the other day, "Yes, I disagree with president, but he's been a great president." Oh, good. Thanks. Thank you very much. Because of him and others. Brian Kemp, vote him the hell out of office, please.

Donald Trump: (53:05)

Well, his rates are so low, his approval rating now, I think it just reached a record low. They've rejected five separate appeals for an independent and comprehensive audit of signatures in Fulton County. Even without an audit, the number of fraudulent ballots that we've identified across the state is staggering. Over 10,300 ballots in Georgia were cast by individuals whose names and dates of birth match Georgia residents who died in 2020 and prior to the election. More than 2,500 ballots were cast by individuals whose names and dates of birth match incarcerated felons in Georgia prison. People who are not allowed to vote. More than 4,500 illegal ballots were cast by individuals who do not appear on the state's own voter rolls. Over 18,000 illegal ballots were cast by individuals who registered to vote using an address listed as vacant, according to the postal service. At least 88,000 ballots in Georgia were cast by people whose registrations were illegally backdated.

Donald Trump: (54:18)

Each one of these is far more than we need. 66,000 votes in Georgia were cast by individuals under the legal voting age. And at least 15,000 ballots were cast by individuals who moved out of the state prior to November 3rd election. They say they moved right back. They move right back. Oh, they moved out. They moved right back. Okay. They miss Georgia that much. I do. I love Georgia, but it's a corrupt system. Despite all of this, the margin in Georgia is only 11,779 votes. Each and every one of these issues is enough to give us a victory in Georgia, a big, beautiful victory. Make no mistake, this selection stolen from you, from me and from the country. And not a single swing state has conducted a comprehensive audit to remove the illegal ballots. This should absolutely occur in every single contestant state before the election is certified.

Donald Trump: (55:21)

In the State of Arizona, over 36,000 ballots were illegally cast by non-citizens. 2000 ballots were returned with no address. More than 22,000 ballots were returned before they were ever supposedly mailed out. They returned, but we haven't mailed them yet. 11,600 more ballots and votes were counted more than there were actual voters. You see that? So you have more votes again than you have voters.

Donald Trump: (55:51)

150,000 people registered in Maya Copa County after the registration deadline. 103,000 ballots in the county were sent for electronic adjudication with no Republican observers. In Clark County, Nevada, the accuracy settings on signature verification machines were purposely lowered before they were used to count over 130,000 ballots. If you signed your name as Santa Claus, it would go through. There were also more than 42,000 double votes in Nevada. Over 150, 000 people were hurt so badly by what took place. And 1500 ballots were cast by individuals whose names and dates of birth match Nevada residents who died in 2020, prior to November 3rd election. More than 8,000 votes were cast by individuals who had no address and probably didn't live there. The margin in Nevada is down at a very low number. Any of these things would have taken care of the situation. We would have won-

Donald Trump: (57:03)

Any of these things would have taken care of the situation. We would have won Nevada also. Every one of these we're going over, we win.

In Michigan quickly, the secretary of state, a real great one, flooded the state with unsolicited mail-in ballot applications, sent to every person on the rolls, in direct violation of state law. More than 17,000 Michigan ballots were cast by individuals whose names and dates of birth matched people who were deceased. In Wayne County, that's a great one. That's Detroit. 174,000 ballots were counted without being tied to an actual registered voter. Nobody knows where they came from. Also in Wayne County, poll watches observed canvassers re-scanning batches of ballots over and over again, up to three or four or five times. In Detroit, turnout was 139% of registered voters. Think of that. So you had 139% of the people in Detroit voting. This is in Michigan, Detroit, Michigan.

Donald Trump: (58:08)

A career employee of the Detroit, City of Detroit, testified under penalty of perjury that she witnessed city workers coaching voters to vote straight Democrat, while accompanying them to watch who they voted for. When a Republican came in, they wouldn't talk to him. The same worker was instructed not to ask for any voter ID and not to attempt to validate any signatures if they were Democrats. She also told to illegally, and was told backdate ballots received after the deadline and reports that thousands and thousands of ballots were improperly backdated. That's Michigan. Four witnesses have testified under penalty of perjury that after officials in Detroit announced the last votes had been counted, tens of thousands of additional ballots arrived without required envelopes. Every single one was for a Democrat. I got no votes.

Donald Trump: (59:10)

At 6:31 AM, in the early morning hours after voting had ended, Michigan suddenly reported 147,000 votes. An astounding 94% went to Joe Biden, who campaigned brilliantly from his basement. Only a couple of percentage points went to Trump. Such gigantic and one-sided vote dumps were only observed in a few swing states and they were observed in the states where it was necessary. You know what's interesting, President Obama beat Biden in every state other than the swing states where Biden killed him. But the swing States were the ones that mattered. There were always just enough to push Joe Biden barely into the lead. We were ahead by a lot and within the number of hours we were losing by a little.

Donald Trump: (01:00:03)

In addition, there is the highly troubling matter of Dominion voting systems. In one Michigan County alone, 6,000 votes were switched from Trump to Biden and the same systems are used in the majority of states in our country. Senator William Ligon, a great gentleman, chairman of Georgia Senate Judiciary Subcommittee, Senator Ligon, highly respected on elections has written a letter describing his concerns with Dominion in Georgia.

Donald Trump: (01:00:40)

He wrote, and I quote, "The Dominion voting machines employed in Fulton County had an astronomical and astounding 93.67% error rate." It's only wrong 93% of the time. "In the scanning of ballots requiring a review panel to adjudicate or determine the voter's interest, in over 106,000 ballots out of a total of 113,000." Think of it, you go in and you vote and then they tell people who you're supposed to be voting for. They make up whatever they want. Nobody's ever even heard. They adjudicate your vote. They say, "Well, we don't think Trump wants to vote for Trump. We think he wants to vote for Biden. Put it down for Biden." The national average for such an error rate is far less than 1% and yet you're at 93%. " The source of this astronomical error rate must be identified to determine if these machines were set up or destroyed to allow for a third party to disregard the actual ballot cast by the registered voter."

Donald Trump: (01:01:44)

The letter continues, "There is clear evidence that tens of thousands of votes were switched from President Trump to former Vice President Biden in several counties in Georgia. For example, in Bibb County, President Trump was reported to have 29, 391 votes at 9:11 PM Eastern time. While simultaneously Vice Spresident Joe Biden was reported to have 17,213. Minutes later, just minutes, at the next update, these vote numbers switched with President Trump going way down to 17,000 and Biden going way up to 29,391." And that was very quick, a 12,000 vote switch, all in Mr. Biden's favor.

Donald Trump: (01:02:31)

So, I mean, I could go on and on about this fraud that took place in every state and all of these legislatures want this back. I don't want to do it to you because I love you and it's freezing out here, but I could just go on forever. I can tell you this...

Speaker 1: (01:02:52)

We love you. We love you. We love you. We love you. We love you. We love you. We love you. We love you.

Donald Trump: (01:03:03)

So when you hear, when you hear, "While there is no evidence to prove any wrongdoing," this is the most fraudulent thing anybody's... This is a criminal enterprise. This is a criminal enterprise and the press will say, and I'm sure they won't put any of that on there because that's no good, do you ever see, "While there is no evidence to back President Trump's assertion," I could go on for another hour reading this stuff to you and telling you about it. There's never been anything like it. Think about it, Detroit had more votes than it had voters. Pennsylvania had 205,000 more votes than it had more, but you don't have to go any... Between that, I think that's almost better than dead people, if you think, right? More votes than they had voters, and many other States are also.

Donald Trump: (01:03:56)

It's a disgrace that the United States of America, tens of millions of people are allowed to go vote without so much as even showing identification. In no state is there any question or effort made to verify the identity, citizenship, residency, or eligibility of the votes cast. The Republicans have to get tougher. You're not going to have a Republican party if you don't get tougher. They want to play so straight, they want to play so, "Sir, yes, the United States, the constitution doesn't allow me to send them back to the States." Well, I say, "Yes, it does because the constitution says you have to protect our country and you have to protect our constitution and you can't vote on fraud," and fraud breaks up everything, doesn't it? When you catch somebody in a fraud, you're allowed to go by very different rules. So I hope Mike has the courage to do what he has to do. And I hope he doesn't listen to the RINOs and the stupid people that he's listening to. It is also widely understood that the voter rolls are crammed full of non-citizens, felons and people who have moved out of state and individuals who are otherwise ineligible to vote. Yet Democrats oppose every effort to clean up their voter rolls. They don't want to clean them up, they are loaded. And how many people here know other people that when the hundreds of thousands and then millions of ballots got sent out, got three, four, five, six, and I heard one who got seven ballots. And then they say, "You didn't quite make it, sir." We won. We won in a landslide. This was a landslide.

Donald Trump: (01:05:43)

They said, "It's not American to challenge the election." This is the most corrupt election in the history, maybe of the world. You know, you could go third world countries, but I don't think they had hundreds of thousands of votes and they don't have voters for them. I mean, no matter where you go, nobody would think this. In fact, it's so egregious, it's so bad, that a lot of people don't even believe it. It's so crazy that people don't even believe it. It can't be true. So they don't believe it. This is not just a matter of domestic politics, this is a matter of national security. So today, in addition to challenging the certification of the election, I'm calling on Congress and the state legislatures to quickly pass sweeping election reforms, and you better do it before we have no country left. Today is not the end. It's just the beginning.

Donald Trump: (01:06:37)

With your help over the last four years, we built the greatest political movement in the history of our country and nobody even challenges that. I say that over and over, and I never get challenged by the fake news, and they challenge almost everything we say. But our fight against the big donors, big media, big tech and others is just getting started. This is the greatest in history. There's never been a movement like that. You look back there all the way to the Washington Monument. It's hard to believe. We must stop the steal and then we must ensure that such outrageous election fraud never happens again, can never be allowed to happen again, but we're going forward. We'll take care of going forward. We got to take care of going back. Don't let them talk, "Okay, well we promise," I've had a lot of people, "Sir, you're at 96% for four years." I said, "I'm not interested right now. I'm interested in right there."

Donald Trump: (01:07:33)
With your help we will finally pass powerful requirements for voter ID. You need an ID to cash your check. You need an ID to go to a bank, to buy alcohol, to drive a car. Every person should need to show an ID in order to cast your most important thing, a vote. We will also require proof of American citizenship in order to vote in American elections. We just had a good victory in court on that one, actually. We will ban ballot harvesting and prohibit the use of unsecured drop boxes to commit rampant fraud. These drop boxes are fraudulent. There for, they get... They disappear and then all of a sudden they show up. It's fraudulent. We will stop the practice of universal, unsolicited mail-in balloting. We will clean up the voter rolls that ensure that every single person who cast a vote is a citizen of our country, a resident of the state in which they vote and their vote is cast in a lawful and honest manner. We will restore the vital civic tradition of in-person voting on election day so that voters can be fully informed when they make their choice. We will finally hold big tech accountable and if these people had courage and guts, they would get rid of Section 230, something that no other company, no other person in America, in the world, has.

Donald Trump: (01:09:10)
All of these tech monopolies are going to abuse their power and interfere in our elections and it has to be stopped and the Republicans have to get a lot tougher and so should the Democrats. They should be regulated, investigated and brought to justice under the fullest extent of the law. They're totally breaking the law. Together we will drain the Washington swamp and we will clean up the corruption in our nation's capital. We have done a big job on it, but you think it's easy, it's a dirty business. It's a dirty business. You have a lot of bad people out there. Despite everything we've been through, looking out all over this country and seeing fantastic crowds, although this I think is our all time record. I think you have 250, 000 people. 250,000.

Donald Trump: (01:10:05)
Looking out at all the amazing patriots here today, I have never been

more confident in our nation's future. Well, I have to say we have to be a little bit careful. That's a nice statement, but we have to be a little careful with that statement. If we allow this group of people to illegally take over our country, because it's illegal when the votes are illegal, when the way they got there is illegal, when the States that vote are given false and fraudulent information. We are the greatest country on earth and we are headed, and were headed, in the right direction. You know, the wall is built, we're doing record numbers at the wall. Now they want to take down the wall. Let's let everyone flow in. Let's let everybody flow in.

Donald Trump: (01:10:52)

We did a great job in the wall. Remember the wall? They said it could never be done. One of the largest infrastructure projects we've ever had in this country and it's had a tremendous impact and we got rid of catch and release, we got rid of all of the stuff that we had to live with. But now the caravans, they think Biden's getting in, the caravans are forming again. They want to come in again and rip off our country. Can't let it happen. As this enormous crowd shows, we have truth and justice on our side. We have a deep and enduring love for America in our hearts. We love our country. We have overwhelming pride in this great country, and we have it deep in our souls. Together we are determined to defend and preserve government of the people, by the people and for the people.

Donald Trump: (01:11:44)

Our brightest days are before us, our greatest achievements still wait. I think one of our great achievements will be election security because nobody until I came along, had any idea how corrupt our elections were. And again, most people would stand there at 9:00 in the evening and say, "I want to thank you very much," and they go off to some other life, but I said, "Something's wrong here. Something's really wrong. Can't have happened." And we fight. We fight like Hell and if you don't fight like Hell, you're not going to have a country anymore.

Donald Trump: (01:12:21)

Our exciting adventures and boldest endeavors have not yet begun. My fellow Americans for our movement, for our children and for our beloved country and I say this, despite all that's happened, the best is yet to come.

Donald Trump: (01:12:43)

So we're going to, we're going to walk down Pennsylvania Avenue, I love Pennsylvania Avenue, and we're going to the Capitol and we're going to try and give... The Democrats are hopeless. They're never voting for anything, not even one vote. But we're going to try and give our Republicans, the weak ones, because the strong ones don't need any of our help, we're going to try and give them the kind of pride and boldness that they need to take back our country.

Donald Trump: (01:13:19)

So let's walk down Pennsylvania Avenue. I want to thank you all. God bless you and God bless America. Thank you all for being here, this is incredible. Thank you very much. Thank you.